THE CATHOLIC UNIVERSITY OF AMERICA
CANON LAW STUDIES

No. 134

p. 21
p

Dowry of Women Religious

A HISTORICAL SYNOPSIS
AND COMMENTARY

A DISSERTATION

*Submitted to the Faculty of the School of Canon
Law of the Catholic University of America in
Partial Fulfillment of the Requirements for
the Degree of Doctor of Canon Law*

Rev. Thomas M. Kealy, A.B., Litt.B., J.C.L.
Priest of the Diocese of Lincoln

THE CATHOLIC UNIVERSITY OF AMERICA PRESS
WASHINGTON, D. C.
1941

*348
K24

NIHIL OBSTAT:

HIERONYMUS D. HANNAN, A.M., S.T.D., LL.B., J.C.D.
Censor Deputatus
Washingtonii, D. C., die XXXI Maii, 1941.

IMPRIMATUR:

✠LUDOVICUS B. KUCERA, D.D., LL.D.
Episcopus Lincolnensis
Lincolniae, Nebraska, die II Junii, 1941.

Copyright 1941
by
THE CATHOLIC UNIVERSITY OF AMERICA PRESS

MURRAY & HEISTER
WASHINGTON, D. C.

PRINTED BY
TIMES AND NEWS PUBLISHING CO.
GETTYSBURG, PA., U. S. A.

To
HIS EXCELLENCY

THE MOST REVEREND LOUIS B. KUCERA, D.D., LL.D.
Bishop of Lincoln

TABLE OF CONTENTS

v

PART II—CANONICAL COMMENTARY

FOREWORD

The purpose of the present work is to offer a study of the canonical legislation on the dowry of women religious. No attempt is made to analyze the constitutions of individual religious institutes, but rather, the study is confined to the general legislation which indicates the tenor after the pattern of which the particular constitutions must be molded.

The work is divided into two distinct parts, the first of which consists in a historical synopsis of the development of religious dowry. Naturally, the clear and precise dotal legislation in the Code of Canon Law is not coexistent with the religious life itself. In fact, dowry as a canonical institution did not make its appearance before the latter part of the sixteenth century—therefore centuries after the establishment of religious community life.

The word "dowry" is a translation of the Latin *"dos."* In Roman Law, as in many modern civil law systems, the *"dos"* consisted in a contribution made by the wife, or by someone else in her behalf, to her husband in view of marriage. The present work is not concerned with marriage dowry, except insofar as the dowry of women religious bears an analogy to it.

In Canon Law the word *"dos"* finds application to three distinct canonical entities: Benefices, pious foundations, and religious institutes of women. *"Dos,"* understood as the material endowment of benefices and pious foundations, is entirely distinct from the dowry of women religious, and therefore is beyond the scope of this treatise.

In the historical synopsis, before treating of canonical legislation on dowry as such, the present work makes a brief study of the repeated and consistent efforts of the Holy See to destroy all vestiges of the crime of simony in the reception of candidates into the religious life.

The second part of the study consists in a commentary on the canons of the Code which pertain to the dowry of women religious.

Throughout the work it is necessary to keep in mind the two principal types of religious institutes, that is, those of solemn vows and those of simple vows, because in some points, especially in the former law, the dotal legislation varied according to the type of institute.

The writer is happy to take this occasion to acknowledge his sincere appreciation and gratitude to the Most Reverend Louis B. Kucera, D.D., LL.D., Bishop of Lincoln, for the opportunity to pursue advanced study. He is also deeply appreciative of the helpful guidance and suggestions offered by the members of the Faculty of the School of Canon Law.

PART I

HISTORICAL SYNOPSIS

CHAPTER I

PRELIMINARY NOTIONS

The definitions given by the various authors for the term *dowry* as referred to institutes of women religious are substantially the same. With only a slight variation of wording these authors understand dowry as a definite sum of money, or its equivalent, paid by a postulant to a convent in which she wishes to make her profession, which money is destined primarily for her support as long as she remains in the institute.[1] As is evident from this definition, the principal purpose of the dowry is to provide a means of support for the religious in the institute in which she has become a member by profession.[2] The dowry, further, serves to provide a dependable financial income by which the convent may enjoy a measure of permanent economic stability.[3] In being relieved from too much solicitude for their material support the religious have a greater opportunity to strive toward spiritual perfection and to devote themselves to the special work of the institute.[4] A third aim is to provide what may be termed an

---

[1] Wernz-Vidal, *Ius Canonicum,* III, *De Religiosis* (Romae, 1933), p. 221, n. 267 (hereafter this work will be cited as *De Religiosis*); Vermeersch-Creusen, *Epitome Iuris Canonici,* I (6. ed., Mechliniae: H. Dessain, 1937), p. 497, n. 698; Augustine, *A Commentary on the New Code of Canon Law,* III, *Religious and Laymen* (5. ed., St. Louis: Herder, 1938), 224; Pellizzarius, *De Monialibus* (Romae, 1761), c. III, sect. II, n. 39; Coronata, *Institutiones Iuris Canonici,* I (2. ed., Taurini: Marietti, 1939), p. 724, n. 577.

[2] Coronata, *loc. cit.*

[3] Battandier, *Guide canonique pour les constitutions des instituts à voeux simples* (6. ed., Paris, 1923), 140; Coronata, *loc. cit.*

[4] Cf. Wernz-Vidal, *op. cit.,* p. 222, n. 267.

1

emergency fund, should the candidate leave the convent.[5] For in this case the present law provides that the entire capital sum of the dowry be restored to her, thus providing a means for her temporary support while she is rehabilitating herself in the world.[6]

Religious dowry received its name from its analogy to the dowry which a woman brings to her husband in marriage.[7] Virgins were from the earliest times called spouses of Christ.[8] United to God as they were by the consecration of their lives, they were considered as having accepted Christ for their Spouse. So real did the Fathers consider the bond of this spiritual matrimony that they called a virgin who had broken her vows an "adulteress."[9] Since the woman who entered a carnal marriage was required to bring a dowry to her husband, it was proper that those virgins who consecrated themselves to Christ should bring a dowry to the monastery in the name of their Spiritual Spouse.[10]

Legal recognition of religious dowry came comparatively late in the history of monasticism. The practice was gradually adopted by monasteries until the Church, appreciating its beneficial effects, eventually approved and regulated it by special canonical legislation.

Several factors contributed to the origin and spread of the canonical institute known as religious dowry. One was the acceptance of more nuns than could be supported from the resources of the convent. Another was the extreme poverty of monasteries, which fact made it necessary in some cases for the

---

[5] Cf. Wernz-Vidal, *op. cit.*, p. 223, n. 268; Coronata, *loc. cit.*; Battandier, *loc. cit.*

[6] Canon 551, § 1.

[7] Cf. Wernz-Vidal, *op. cit.*, p. 222, n. 267; Boudinhon, "Dower,"—*Catholic Encyclopedia*, V, 146.

[8] Cf. St. Athanasius, *Apologia ad Constantium*—Migne, *Patrologiae Cursus Completus, Series Graeca* (Parisiis, 1856-1866), XXV, 639; hereafter this work will be cited as *MPG;* cf. also c. 10, C. XXVII, q. 1.

[9] St. Cyprian, *Ep. 62*—Migne, *Patrologiae Cursus Completus, Series Latina* (Parisiis, 1844-1864), IV, 370; hereafter this work will be cited as *MPL;* St. Augustine, *De Bono Viduitatis*, c. 11—*MPL*, XL, 439; St. Ambrose, *De Lapsu Virginis Consecratae*, lib. I, c. 5—*MPL*, XVI, 373.

[10] Thomassinus, *Vetus et Nova Ecclesiae Disciplina Circa Beneficia et Beneficiarios* (Moguntiae, 1787), pars III, lib. I, c. 51, n. 4; hereafter this work will be cited as Thomassinus; Battandier, *op. cit.*, p. 138.

nuns to leave the cloister and seek support elsewhere.[11] A third factor grew out of certain abuses in the days when admission was gratuitous. Many parents forced some of their daughters to enter a convent, thereby leaving a greater inheritance to the other children.[12]

---

[11] Cabassutius, *Theoria et Praxis Juris Canonici* (Lugduni, 1678), lib. V, c. V, nn. 13, 18; Boudinhon, "Dower,"—*Catholic Encyclopedia*, V, 146.

[12] Cf. Schaefer, *De Religiosis* (3. ed., Roma: S. A. L. E. R., 1940), p. 500, n. 228; Wernz-Vidal, *De Religiosis*, p. 222, footnote 16; Kober, *Die Suspension* (Tübingen, 1862), p. 361.

CHAPTER II

Historical Background of Canonical Legislation on Dowry

ARTICLE I. EARLY MONASTIC RULES

From apostolic times there were virgins and widows who consecrated themselves to God and who devoted their lives to the service of others or to the pursuance of spiritual perfection.[1] During the first three centuries of the Christian era, when there were no convents or monasteries these holy women, consecrated to God by a vow of perpetual chastity, lived in the home of their parents. In the beginning of the fourth century when the fury of the persecutions had subsided and greater freedom of action had been given to the Church, monasteries were built where these women took up residence to pursue spiritual perfection in community life.[2]

The fourth century marked the beginning and rapid spread of the cenobitical life in the Church. Its cradle was in Egypt where Christian monasticism was born.[3] As monasteries of men were established similar houses were founded for women, who imitated the holy zeal and austere life of the monks.[4]

St. Pachomius (292-346) is credited with being the founder not only of the first Christian monastery for men, but also of the first monastery for women. In 328 he established his community on the banks of the Nile at Tabennisi near Denerah.[5]

---

[1] Cf. I Timothy, V, 9; I Corinthians, VII, 25; Acts, XXI, 9; St. Ignatius, *Epistola ad Polycarpum,* c. 5—*MPG,* V, 723; Schaefer, *De Religiosis,* p. 28, n. 13; Steiger, "De Propagatione et Diffusione Vitae Religiosae,"—*Periodica de re Canonica et Morali,* XIII (1924), (37)-(43).

[2] Montalembert, *The Monks of the West* (New York, 1860), I, 189; Thomassinus, pars III, lib. I, c. 51, n. 4.

[3] Cf. Vermeersch, *De Religiosis Institutis et Personis* (4. ed., 2 vols., Brugis, 1907-1909), II, (6).

[4] Cf. Montalembert, *op. cit.,* I, 171.

[5] Steiger, "De Propagatione et Diffusione Vitae Religiosae,"—*op. cit.,* (46).

The first monastery which he established for women was situated across a river from the monastery for men. He placed his sister in charge of the nuns, who carried on many of the same occupations as the monks. They prayed in common, performed the ordinary household duties, and worked in the garden as well as at other manual labor.[6] The rule of Pachomius determined the mode of life for those who had chosen to live under his direction. It provided that no money or presents be taken from those who entered, lest this might be a source of vanity to the rich or of false shame to the poor.[7]

St. Pachomius' foundation of Christian monasticism in Egypt was followed shortly after by a more perfect form of cenobitical life in the East. St. Basil (329-379) inaugurated monasticism in Pontus near Neo-Caesarea after he had made a tour of the monasteries then existing in Egypt, Palestine, Mesopotamia and Syria.[8] A summary of his instructions and advice to those who followed the cenobitical life is contained in his two sets of questions and answers called *Regulae Fusius Tractatae,*[9] and *Regulae Brevius Tractatae.*[10] St. Basil demanded from the novice a renunciation of self and property in accordance with the Gospel precept: "Go sell whatsoever thou hast, and give to the poor, and thou shalt have treasure in heaven; and come, follow me."[11] In prescribing that the novice dispose of his goods to the poor St. Basil does not explicitly forbid the monastery to accept some of these goods, but this seems to be implied by his language.[12]

St. Augustine of Hippo (354-430) organized community life in his African diocese.[13] He stated that the candidates for admission should, if they had possessions in the world, transfer

---

[6] Allies, *The Monastic Life* (London, 1896), 2-3.
[7] Allies, *loc. cit.*
[8] Currier, *History of Religious Orders* (New York, 1894), 77.
[9] *MPG,* XXXI, 906-1051.
[10] *MPG,* XXXI, 1079-1306.
[11] Mark, X, 21.
[12] *Regulae Fusius Tractatae,* VIII and IX—*MPG,* XXXI, 934-943; cf. *Regula Commentata—MPL,* LXVI, 833.
[13] Steiger, "De Propagatione et Diffusione Vitae Religiosae,"—*op. cit.,* (74)-(75).

them to the monastery upon entering. This was not to be understood as restricting admission to the rich, for in the same letter
he warned the members who had been poor and without possessions in the world not to seek them in the monastery.[14]

St. Caesarius (470-543), Bishop of Arles, composed two monastic rules, one for men and one for women. The latter was
the first rule drawn up explicitly for women living the perfect
community life. In the first chapter of his rule for monks St.
Caesarius forbids anyone to be received into the monastery who
had not first carried out the precept of Christ: "If thou wilt
be perfect, go sell what thou hast, and give to the poor. . . ."[15]
He added that if the novice did not wish to distribute all his
goods to the poor, he could give some to his parents or to the
monastery.[16] The same renunciation was required in chapter 4
of his rule for virgins, with the exception that he did not explicitly state that the novice could donate her goods to the
monastery.[17]

St. Benedict (480-543) founded his first monastery at Subiaco,
and later the famous monastery at Monte Cassino. It was near
this abbey that his sister, St. Scholastica, who had consecrated
herself to God from her infancy, presided over a group of nuns.
She became the patroness and model of the large family of virgins
who were to acknowledge, adopt, and follow the rule of her
brother.[18] According to chapter 58 of the Benedictine rule the
monastery was permitted to accept any offerings made by the
novice in the disposal of his worldly goods.[19] It was not obligatory, however, for the novice to make a donation to the monastery. Chapter 59 provided that those who had little or no property,
and therefore were unable to make an offering, should be received
simply by the offering of their petition.[20]

---

[14] *Epistola CCXI*, n. 5—*MPL*, XXXIII, 960.
[15] Matthew XIX, 21.
[16] *Regula ad Monachos*, c. I—*MPL*, LXVII, 1099.
[17] *Regula ad Virgines—MPL*, LXVII, 1107-1108.
[18] Montalembert, *op. cit.*, I, 325.
[19] Butler, *Sancti Benedicti Regula Monasteriorum* (2. ed., Friburgi
Brisgoviae: Herder, 1927), 105-110.
[20] Butler, *op. cit.*, 110-111.

In the early days of monasticism, most of the leaders drew up lists of instructions for use in their own monasteries. Therefore, uniformity of discipline and practice could hardly be expected. John Cassian (c. 360-435), who visited Egypt, Palestine and Mesopotamia before establishing a monastery in Gaul, wrote that he found almost as many rules as there were monasteries.[21] The early rules for the most part were similar to that of St. Benedict in permitting donations to the monastery by the novice.[22] There were two notable exceptions. John Cassian, in writing of the Egyptian monks, gave several reasons why they did not accept the novices' goods. He said it would tend to engender a lack of equality among the monks, be harmful to the spirit of humility, and create a state of tepidity.[23] The rule of St. Fructuosus (+c. 665) was the other exception. Stressing the literal fulfillment of the words of Christ, St. Fructuosus stated that the novice should distribute his goods to the poor. The rule expressly forbade the monastery to accept any material goods from the novice, even though they be offered voluntarily.[24]

In summing up one's appraisal of the early monastic rules, one may safely conclude that the great majority of them permitted the novice, in disposing of his goods, to bestow material gifts upon the monastery, and allowed the monastery to accept such donations. It is important to note that none of the rules went so far as to demand anything that could be construed as a price of admission to the religious state.[25]

---

[21] Allies, *op. cit.*, 102.

[22] ". . . non desunt tamen, et quidem majori numero monachorum regulae, quae Benedictinae concinant, ut Regula SS. Serapionis, Macarii, Paphnutii, et alterius Macarii, Regula tertia SS. Patrum, S. Caesarii, S. Aureliani Tarnatensis, S. Isidori, et Magistri."—*Regula Commentata—MPL*, LXVI, 833.

[23] *De Coenobiorum Institutis,* lib. IV, c. 4—*MPL*, XLIX, 156-157.

[24] C. 18—*MPL*, LXXXVII, 1125.

[25] Thomassinus, pars III, lib. I, c. 50, n. 3; cf. Leinz "Die Supernumerarier in den Klöstern,"—*Archiv für katholisches Kirchenrecht*, LXXIX (1899), 55-56.

ARTICLE II. ROMAN LAW

Considerable legislation is found in Roman Law on marriage dowry but none on the dowry of women religious as such, although some enactments, especially that of Novel 123.38,[26] bear a close resemblance to it.

The institution of the dowry of women religious in the canon law sources did not make its appearance until the sixteenth century. In the ecclesiastical legislation for religious institutes of men there has never been any question of bringing a dowry, although it was permitted for the monastery, if it was poor, to demand that those entering bring something to help pay for their support.[27]

Roman Law contained certain provisions pertaining to the property of those who entered or left the religious life. The Emperor Justinian (527-565) declared that it was unlawful for parents to prevent their children from entering the religious life, and further, that parents could not exclude their children who had entered monasteries from their rightful inheritance. In the event that the parents died intestate their property was to be divided according to the provisions of law. And the children who had entered the religious life were to receive the same share in the property of their deceased parents as they would if they had remained in the world. In other words, entrance into a monastery did not affect a person's legal right of inheritance. But if afterwards anyone left the monastic life, his property was to remain with the monastery.[28]

In 535 Justinian enacted a law which permitted a person entering the religious life to dispose of his property in any way that he wished. All his goods which had not been disposed of before his entrance became the property of the monastery. If he had children, however, there was a restriction on his freedom in the distribution of his property. The law required that he leave at least one-fourth of his estate to his children. If he had a wife and left her to enter a monastery, he was to refund the

---

[26] Cf. *infra*, p. 9.
[27] Cf. Wernz-Vidal, *De Religiosis*, p. 222, n. 267.
[28] C (1.3) 54.

marriage dowry to her and whatever else had been agreed upon in case of his death. Justinian added that the provisions of this law applied not only to monks, but also to women who took up the monastic life.[29]

Another legislative enactment in 535 restated a former law which provided that if a monk gave up the monastic life the property which he possessed upon his entrance had to be left with the monastery.[30]

Two separate laws, one in 535 and the other in 546, provided that if a monk transferred from one monastery to another, the property which he possessed was to be left with the first monastery.[31]

In 546 Justinian changed the former law of 535 somewhat by stating that if a man or woman embraced the monastic life and had no children, the monastery was entitled to his or her estate. If such persons had children and had not disposed of their property before entering the monastery, they were to do so even after entering. Whatever was not distributed to the children became the property of the monastery, provided, however, that the children were first given the share to which they were entitled. If the person who entered the monastic life desired to distribute all his property to his children, the law required that he reserve a portion of it for the monastery. Finally, if he should die before having divided his estate, the children were to be given their lawful portion, and the remainder became the property of the monastery.[32]

ARTICLE III.   LEGISLATION AGAINST SIMONY

A. *The II Council of Nice (787)*

With the lapse of time avarice and greed had taken their toll among the monks and nuns in monasteries. Simoniacal abuses were severely condemned in the II Council of Nice (787), which

---

[29] N (5.5).
[30] N (5.4).
[31] N (5.7) ; N (123.42).
[32] N (123.38).

was the VII General Council of the Church. Canon 19 of this
Council stated:

> Avarice has made such inroads among the rulers of
> Churches that some of them, calling themselves religious
> men and women, demand money from those who present
> themselves for the sacerdotal order and the monastic
> life. . . . If the offender be a *hegumena* (abbess), she
> shall be removed from her monastery and placed in
> another in a subordinate position. . . . With regard to
> what has been given by parents to their children in the
> monastery as a dowry, or what such persons themselves
> have contributed from their own means, with a declara-
> tion that such gifts are made to God, we have decided
> that whether such persons continue in the monastery or
> not, the gifts are to remain with the monastery in ac-
> cordance with their original declaration; unless there be
> good ground for complaint against the superior (for a
> person's departure).[33]

This canon of the Council of Nice contains a number of
important points regarding the origin of canonical legislation on
religious dowry. First of all, it forbade the monastery to exact
any payment on the occasion of the entrance of a candidate.
All authors agree that simony in defiance of the divine law would
be committed if the monastery demanded a price for admission
to the religious state. In spite of the vigorous denunciation of
the practice of demanding a price from the candidate, the Council
sanctioned voluntary offerings made by the parents for their
children after the manner of a dowry. Such offerings could
be given by the parents and accepted by the monastery, but if
they were not offered voluntarily the monastery could not demand
them. Furthermore, the voluntary offerings, when once made,
became the property of the monastery and were not returned
if the candidate should later return to the world. An exception
was made to the retention of the dowry by the monastery if the
superior was responsible for the departure of the religious.

---

[33] Mansi, *Sacrorum Conciliorum Nova et Amplissima Collectio* (Parisiis,
1901-1927), XIII, 436; translation from Schroeder, *Disciplinary Decrees
of the General Councils* (St. Louis: Herder, 1937), pp. 152-153.

These principles were adopted in substance by numerous particular councils and were urged by decrees of the Roman Pontiffs for centuries afterwards. The Council of Nice cited the avarice of the religious superiors as the cause for the abuse. An attempt on the part of the superiors to excuse their practice on the grounds of poverty of the monastery was met by legislation in numerous councils which forbade the superiors to admit more candidates than could be supported by the ordinary revenue of the monastery.[34] By thus limiting the number of religious in accordance with the resources of the institution, the superiors could no longer allege the excuse of poverty for exacting payments from the new candidates on the occasion of their admission.

B. *The Decretum Gratiani*

In the *Decree of Gratian* the author discussed the question of whether it was lawful to exact money for entrance into a monastery. His conclusion corresponded with the law of the II Council of Nice when he stated that nothing could be demanded, but whatever was offered voluntarily could be accepted by the monastery.[35]

C. *The Decretals*

Several chapters of the Decretals contain legislation against simoniacal practices of monasteries. In the Council of Tours (1163) Alexander III (1159-1181) issued a prohibition against demanding money from those who wished to enter religion,[36]

---

[34] Cf. VI Council of Arles (813), canon 8: "Ut non amplius suscipiantur in monasterio canonicorum, atque monachorum, seu etiam puellarum, nisi quantum ratio permittit, et in eodem monasterio absque necessariarum rerum penuria degere possunt."—Harduin, *Acta Conciliorum et Epistolae Decretales ac Constitutiones Summorum Pontificum* (Parisiis, 1715), IV, 1004 (hereafter this work will be cited as Harduin). The text of this law was later given universal binding force by its inclusion in the Decretals of Gregory IX, C. 1, X, *de institutionibus*, III, 7. Similar legislation was enacted in the following particular councils: Council of Mainz (813), canon 19—Harduin, IV, 1013; Council of Tours (813), canon 31—Harduin, IV, 1027.

[35] C. I. q. 2 (*dictum Gratiani*).

[36] C. 6—Mansi, XXI, 1178; c. 8, X, *de simonia*, V, 3.

and the same Pontiff repeated the prohibition in a particular case which was brought to his attention.[37]

Among the disciplinary measures adopted by the III General Council of the Lateran (1179) was a prohibition which forbade monasteries to receive new members for a price. The sanction provided that anyone who had paid to enter should not be promoted to orders, and that those who received such a one should be deprived of their offices.[38]

The attitude of the supreme pontiffs toward the practice of demanding money from entrants into religion is seen from a letter of Pope Innocent III (1198-1216) to the Archbishop of Canterbury. After it was discovered that in this archdiocese a great many had been received into monasteries by the payment of a price Innocent was asked whether, in view of the number, the rigor of the law could be somewhat relaxed. He replied that in spite of the large number thus received the full severity of the law had to be exercised against the guilty. In conformity with previous legislation he added that voluntary offerings were permitted.[39] The same Pontiff issued a decree to the bishops of France condemning the widespread and detestable abuse whereby monasteries of men and women demanded money from their prospective members. Innocent commanded the bishops of France to take effective means to eradicate the abuse.[40] The Council of Rouen (1214) mentioned the special mandate of Innocent and condemned simoniacal entrance into religion.[41]

The particular legislation enacted by Innocent III was climaxed by the action of the IV General Council of the Lateran in 1215. This Council revealed that the abuse of demanding money from girls entering monasteries was so common that it tainted the reception of almost every nun. The practice received the vigorous condemnation of the Council in the following words:

---

[37] C. 19, X, *de simonia*, V, 3.
[38] C. 10—Hefele-LeClercq, *Histoire des Conciles* (Paris, 1907-1938), V, 1096; c. 2, X, *de statu monachorum*, III, 35.
[39] C. 30, X, *de simonia*, V, 3.
[40] Const. *"Multotiens audivimus,"* 17 apr. 1210—*Bull. Rom.*, III, 246.
[41] C. 1—Mansi, XXII, 905.

Since the stain of simony has so infected many nuns that scarcely any are received into the community without a price, doing this on the plea of poverty to conceal that evil, we strictly forbid that this be done in the future, decreeing that whoever in the future shall be guilty of such irregularity, both the one receiving and the one received, whether subject or superioress, shall, without hope of restoration, be removed from their monastery to one of stricter observance to do penance for the remainder of their life. Those nuns, however, who have been so received before the publication of this decree, are to be removed from the monasteries which they entered in a wrong manner and placed in others of the same order. . . .[42]

When Urban IV (1261-1264) learned of what he called the detestable abuse of demanding money and other temporal goods from the candidates for admission to monasteries, he restated the former canons forbidding such practices. In addition, he inflicted the penalty of excommunication reserved to the Apostolic See upon those who gave and those who received these payments. Only that which was offered voluntarily and without any stain of simony could be accepted by the monastery.[43]

The foregoing legislation of the Decretals was directed toward the eradication of simony. An attempt was made to abolish everything that resembled the exchange of religious profession for a temporal price. Increasingly severe sanctions were added to the laws in an effort to curb the evil which had its origin in many cases in the avarice of unworthy religious superiors. No distinction was made in the laws between the price paid for admission to the religious state and the compensation paid for the support of the monk or nun. This led some writers to the conclusion that under no title whatsoever could a monastery

---

[42] C. 64—Hefele-LeClercq, V, 1384; c. 40, X, *de simonia,* V, 3; translation by Schroeder, *Disciplinary Decrees of the General Councils,* 288.

[43] C. 1, *de simonia,* V, 1, in Extravag. com.; cf. Fuchs, "Rückgabe der Mitgift an die ausscheidende Klosterfrau,"—*ThPrQs,* LXXXVIII (1935), 359-360.

exact money from a candidate.[44] The majority of writers, however, contended that the prohibitions did not extend to legitimate
payments for the support of the members. These writers ex-
amined the laws one by one, especially that of the IV General
Lateran Council and showed that it was not the mind of the
legislator to forbid payments to the monastery for the support
of the professed religious if the monastery lacked the income
to bear this expense.[45]

The justification for such payments was explained by St.
Thomas. He stated that it was unlawful to exact or receive
anything as a price for entrance to the religious life. But if
the monastery lacked sufficient resources, it was lawful, while
entrance to the monastery remained free, to accept something for
the support of those who were about to be received.[46]

St. Bonaventure arrived at a similar conclusion and said that
when a person is received on account of the money he pays
it is simony, because the spiritual reception is purchased with
a temporal price. But when the money is received from a person
who would be received freely if the monastery were able to
support him there is no simony as long as the form corresponds
to the intention.[47]

---

[44] Cf. Van-Espen, *Jus Ecclesiasticum Universum* (Lovanii, 1753), *De
Vitio Peculiaritatis,* pars II, c. IV, nn. 1-5.
[45] Cf. *Glossa* of Joannes Andreae to *paupertatis* of c. 40, X, *de simonia,*
V, 3; Gonzalez-Tellez, *Commentaria Perpetua in Singulos Textus quinque
Librorum Decretalium Gregorii* IX (Venetiis, 1699), tom. IV, lib. V, tit.
III, nn. 6-7; Fagnanus, *Commentarium in Librum Decretalium* (Venetiis,
1709), lib. III, *de institutionibus,* c. I, nn. 24-25; Gibalinus, *De Simonia
Universa Tractatio Theologica et Canonica* (Lugduni, 1659), q. 18, consect.
IX; Cabassutius, *Theoria et Praxis Juris Canonici,* lib. V, c. V, nn. 1-3;
Petra, *Commentaria ad Constitutiones Apostolicas* (Venetiis, 1729), tom.
III, const. XII, Innocentii IV (*Solet annuere*), sect. I, nn. 16-28 (hereafter this work will be cited as *Commentaria*); Benedict XIV, *De Synodo
Dioecesana* (Romae, 1788), lib. XI, c. VI, nn. 1-6; Reiffenstuel, *Ius Canonicum Universum* (Parisiis, 1864-1870), lib. V, tit. III, nn. 163-166; Santi-
Leitner, *Praelectiones Juris Canonici* (4. ed., Ratisbonae, 1903-1905), lib. V,
tit. III, nn. 55-58.
[46] *Summa Theologica,* II-II, q. 100, art. 3, ad 4.
[47] *Opera Omnia* (Quaracchi ed. 1882-1902), VIII, *Determinationes Quaestionum circa Regulam Fratrum Minorum,* opusculum XIII, pars II, q. 18.

D. *Particular Councils*

Particular councils in the fifteenth century, calling attention to previous canonical legislation against simony, strictly forbade monasteries to demand a price from, or to enter into pecuniary pacts with, candidates. Customs to the contrary were branded as corruptions of law.[48]

The Council of Sens in 1528 set forth very definite rules regulating the reception of nuns into monasteries. Decree 28 prescribed that only that number be admitted which could be supported by the monastery. Nothing, under pretext of custom or any other title, could be demanded from nuns admitted within this fixed number. The same decree added that if any other candidates over and above this group wished to join, they could be admitted if they brought a pension sufficient to provide for their support.[49] According to Thomassinus the doctrine and will of the Church regarding religious dowry was explained most clearly in this Council. He stated that the Council of Sens prescribed in different words that which previous councils had wished when they ordered the number of nuns to be fixed for each monastery.[50]

---

[48] Cf. Council of Paris (1429), can. 15—Mansi, XXVIII, 1104; Council of Freising (1440), c. 12—Mansi, XXXII, 9; Council of Soissons (1456)—Mansi, XXXII, 182; Council of Sens (1485), art. III, c. III—Mansi, XXXII, 426; Council of Salzburg (1490), c. *"De Monialibus Deo Devotis,"*—Mansi, XXXII, 508.

[49] "Si qua tamen ultra eas in hujusmodi monasteriis se recipi petat, id non interdicimus, dummodo congruam secum afferat pensionem, qua cum ceteris religiosis numerariis alatur. Non tamen in locum numerariarum succedat; sed decedentibus numerariis aliae novae et pauperes subrogentur."—Mansi, XXXII, 1195.

[50] Pars III, lib. I, c. 54, n. 2.

CHAPTER III

Dowry for Monasteries Whose Members Took Solemn Vows

The legislation on the dowry for nuns (*moniales*) with solemn vows preceded, and was distinct from, the legislation for sisters (*sorores*) with simple vows. Therefore, in a historical study of canonical legislation on religious dowry care must be taken to distinguish between that which applies to the former and that which applies to the latter type of religious body. For this reason the present chapter deals exclusively with the legislation pertaining to institutes of solemn vows, while the following chapter will be devoted to those of simple vows.

ARTICLE I. THE COUNCIL OF TRENT

The Council of Trent (1545-1563) enacted no explicit legislation on religious dowry. The canons of the Council repeated the legislation of preceding centuries, forbidding the reception of more members than could be supported from the income or the customary alms (*consuetae eleemosynae*) received by the monastery.[1] Just what was included in the term *ex consuetis eleemosynis* (from the customary alms) is not certain. Some authors hold that the Council, in this phrase, approved the payment of a dowry. They say that the *consuetae eleemosynae* included the dotal offerings from the candidates seeking admission.[2]

---

[1] "In praedictis autem monasteriis et domibus, tam virorum quam mulierum, bona immobilia possidentibus vel non possidentibus, is tantum numerus constituatur ac in posterum conservetur, qui ex redditibus propriis monasteriorum, vel ex consuetis eleemosynis commode possit sustentari."— Sessio XXV, *de regularibus et monialibus,* c. 3.

[2] Cf. Pennacchi, *Commentaria in Constitutionem Apostolicae Sedis* (Romae, 1883), tom. I, appendix XXIV, 911, 918; (hereafter this work will be cited as *Commentaria*); Thomassinus, pars III, lib. I, c. 54, nn. 3, 7; Zallinger, *Institutiones Juris Ecclesiastici* (Romae, 1823), lib. V, tit. III, n. 93.

16

Another law enacted by the Council of Trent had an indirect bearing on religious dowry. This law forbade the acceptance by the monastery of anything from the novice other than the cost of food and clothing during the time of the novitiate.[3] Other gifts made by the novice would not be simoniacal of themselves, but the Council forbade them in order to safeguard the freedom of the novice.[4] Nothing is stated in this law concerning payment for the support of the member *after* profession. Nor does the Council forbid voluntary offerings, except as stated in the case of novices.

ARTICLE II. THE I AND II PROVINCIAL COUNCILS OF
MILAN—1565 AND 1569

A new era in the history of dowry of women religious was inaugurated by St. Charles Borromeo in the I and II Provincial Councils of Milan. St. Charles, who had attended the Council of Trent, was regarded as a most reliable interpreter of the canons of that important Council.[5] Because of his enactments in these two Provincial Councils he is considered to be the first author of a law exacting a dowry from women entering religion.[6]

In the I Provincial Council of Milan (1565) it was decreed that before a nun could be clothed with the religious habit she must have first deposited with a reliable person a sum of money

---

[3] "Sed neque ante professionem, excepto victu et vestitu novitii vel novitiae illius temporis, quo in probatione est, quocumque praetextu, a parentibus, vel propinquis, aut curatoribus eius, monasterio aliquid ex bonis eiusdem tribuatur; ne hac occasione discedere nequeat, quod totam, vel maiorem partem substantiae suae monasterium possideat, nec facile si discesserit, id recuperare possit."—Sessio XXV, *de regularibus et monialibus*, c. 16.

[4] Bouix, *Tractatus de Jure Regularium* (3. ed., Parisiis, 1882), tom. I, pars IV, sect. III, c. III, q. II.

[5] Cf. Benedict XIV, *De Synodo Dioecesana*, tom. XI, c. 6, n. 5; Thomassinus, pars III, lib. I, c. 54, n. 3.

[6] Wernz-Vidal, *De Religiosis*, p. 221, footnote 12; Coronata, *Institutiones*, I, p. 724, n. 577; Kober, *Die Suspension*, 362; Fuchs, "Rückgabe der Mitgift an die ausscheidende Klosterfrau,"—*ThPrQs*, LXXXVIII (1935), 360.

to be given to the monastery after profession for her support.[7]
The money had to be deposited at the beginning of the novitiate,
but it could not be given to the monastery until after the profession. A trustworthy person received the deposit from the
novice, took care of it during the period of the novitiate, and
then, after the profession of the girl, transferred it to the
monastery. This deposit was entirely distinct from, and in addition
to, that sum which was permitted by the Council of Trent to be
paid by the novice for her food and clothing during the period
of the novitiate.

The II Provincial Council of Milan (1569) confirmed the
above legislation. It further prescribed that the bishop designate
in each case the amount of money which was to constitute the
dowry. Considerable discretionary powers were conferred upon
the bishop in this matter, as he could dispense from the payment
altogether if, in his judgment, the income of the monastery was
sufficient to make the payment unnecessary.[8]

A comparison between the Council of Sens in 1528,[9] and these
two Provincial Councils of Milan, in 1565 and 1569 respectively,
shows that they worked toward the same end but by slightly
different routes. According to the Council of Sens a designated
number—called numerary nuns—was admitted free. Others—
called supernumerary nuns—were admitted only if they gave
a just payment in compensation for their support. The Councils

---

[7] "Quod professione facta, eleemosynae gratia ad professam sustentandam
monasterio datur, id quo tempore puella religionis habitum suscipiet, apud
virum, monialibus et earum superiori probatum, deponatur, ut nullo im-
pedimento tum monialibus praesto esse possit."—Ratti, *Acta Ecclesiae
Mediolanensis ab eius Initiis usque ad Nostram Aetatem* (Mediolani, 1890),
II, 136; c. 6—Mansi, XXXIV, 84.

[8] "Episcopus praetera tum impensas aestimet, quae et in religionis ingressu,
et tempore professionis fieri solent pro vestitu, aut pro aliis rebus, ad ipsius
puellae, vel monasterii usum commoditatemve pertinentibus; tum pecuniae
etiam summam prescribit, quam puella alimentorum nomine monasterio
det; nisi census, aut alia bona immobilia, quorum annui fructus, eiusdem
iudicio, ad ea alimenta satis sint, monasterio attribuantur."—Ratti, *Acta
Ecclesiae Mediolanensis, Capita Quaedam ad Moniales Pertinentia*, c. II,
vol. II, pp. 201-202; Mansi, XXXIV, 130.

[9] *Supra*, p. 15.

of Milan, however, made no distinction between numerary and supernumerary nuns. In prescribing the amount to be paid by the candidates the bishop took into account the financial condition of the monastery as well as the ability of the girl to pay.[10]

A number of other particular councils which were held toward the end of the sixteenth century followed one or the other of these two plans. For example, the Council of Rheims (1583)[11] and the Council of Avignon (1594)[12] followed the legislation of Milan, while the Council of Tours (1583)[13] followed that of the Council of Sens.[14]

The Provincial Council of Mexico in 1585 seemed to imply the approval of religious dowry when it prescribed the type of investment to be made of funds paid on the occasion of the entrance of candidates into a monastery.[15]

A uniform practice at this early date was not prescribed by the Holy See, nor was the observance the same in all monasteries. For example, in the same year as the First Council of Milan (1585) the Council of Cambrai, France, strictly forbade pecuniary pacts, and *all* payments by the candidate, even that which was given for support.[16]

ARTICLE III. NECESSITY OF THE DOWRY

Within a decade after the Council of Trent and the Provincial Councils of Milan legislative enactments on monastic dowry emanated directly from the Holy See. A rigid law for universal application was not immediately set forth. The Holy See preferred to observe the practicality of the different methods employed in various monasteries, and from these gradually to formu-

---

[10] Thomassinus, pars III, lib. I, c. 54, n. 6.
[11] Tit. *de simoniacis et fiduciariis,* c. 10—Mansi, XXXIV, 710.
[12] Tit. 50—Mansi, XXXIV, 1359.
[13] Mansi, XXXIV, 846.
[14] Thomassinus, pars III, lib. I, c. 54, n. 8; Benedict XIV, *De Synodo Dioecesana,* lib. XI, c. VI, n. 5.
[15] C. 4—Mansi, XXXIV, 1119.
[16] C. 10—Mansi, XXXIII, 1418.

late a policy which would be the most effective in the accomplish-
ment of the purpose of the dowry.[17]

The dotal legislation of the Holy See was developed through
the responses given by the Sacred Congregations to individual
questions presented for solution. The Holy See studied carefully the different methods represented on the one hand by the
Council of Sens, and on the other by the two Provincial Councils
of Milan. The plan of the former in admitting the numerary
nuns without any payment, and requiring a dowry only from
the supernumerary members had its advantages, but the study
and experience of the Sacred Congregations inclined them to
prefer the plan originated by St. Charles Borromeo, namely, of
requiring a dowry from all who were admitted, that is, from the
numerary as well as from the supernumerary nuns.[18]

A. *Supernumerary Nuns*

During the period immediately following the Council of Trent
the Holy See was insistent that a designated number of nuns
be established for each monastery, as had been ordered by the
Council.[19] Investiture and profession were forbidden by the
Sacred Congregation of Bishops and Regulars in those monasteries
for which the number had not been determined.[20] Permission

---

[17] Cf. Battandier, *Guide canonique,* p. 138.

[18] Benedict XIV, *De Synodo Dioecesana,* tom. XI, c. 6, n. 5; Fuchs,
"Rückgabe der Mitgift an die ausscheidende Klosterfrau,"—*ThPrQs,*
LXXXVIII (1935), 360.

[19] Sessio XXV, *de regularibus et monialibus,* c. 3; cf. Pius V, const.
"Circa," 29 maii 1566—Bizzarri, *Collectanea in Usum Secretariae S. C.
Episcoporum et Regularium* (2. ed., Romae, 1885), p. 207; Gregory XIII,
const. *"Deo Sacris,"* 30 dec. 1572—Bizzarri, *loc. cit.;* S. C. Ep. et Reg.,
Portugallien., 6 iun. 1605—Bizzarri, *op. cit.,* p. 334; decr. S. C. Ep. et Reg.,
6 sept. 1604—Bizzarri, *op. cit.,* p. 241 (hereafter this work will be cited as
Coll. S. C. Ep. et Reg.).

[20] S. C. Ep. et Reg., *Tricaricen.,* 3 febr. 1602—Ferraris, *Prompta
Bibliotheca Canonica, Juridica, Moralis, Theologica, necnon Ascetica,
Polemica, Rubristica, Historica,* "Moniales," II, n. 13; S. C. Ep. et Reg.,
Reatina, 6 aug. 1602—Ferraris, *loc. cit.;* S. C. Ep. et Reg., *Interamenen.,*
16 mart. 1604—Ferraris, *loc. cit.* (hereafter this work will be cited as
Ferraris).

was granted to admit supernumerary nuns provided they paid a *double* dowry. This double dowry consisted in twice the sum required from those who were admitted within the established number of members for the respective monastery. In no instance, however, could the double dowry amount to a sum less than 400 *scudi*. The supernumerary nuns always remained supernumerary, although in all else they were equal to the other nuns in the monastery. Upon the death of a nun who had been received as a numerary member, her place could not be assigned to one of the supernumerary nuns, but was to be filled by a new member who would be admitted with the ordinary—not the double—dowry.[21]

A double dowry was also prescribed by the Holy See if a third daughter of one family was to be admitted as a numerary member in the same monastery. If such a one sought to be admitted as a supernumerary she was required to pay a *triple* dowry.[22]

B. *Numerary Nuns*

The lawfulness of exacting a dowry from nuns who were received over and above the defined number for the monastery was readily admitted. Under the presumption that the monastery was unable to support them, it was in harmony with the doctrine advanced by St. Thomas, St. Bonaventure, and others, to permit the monastery to demand from these candidates a sum of money sufficient to provide for their material sustenance. This same principle found application in regard to *all* candidates admitted into monasteries which were poor. If the money exacted from those who entered was not a price of admission to the religious state, but rather a contribution for the support of the members

[21] S. C. Ep. et Reg., decr. 6 sept. 1604—Bizzarri, *op. cit.*, 241-243; decr. 2 iun. 1602—Barbosa, *Iuris Ecclesiastici Universi Libri Tres* (Lugduni, 1660), lib. I, c. 44, n. 34; cf. Leinz, "Die Supernumerarier in den Klöstern," —*AKKR*, LXXIX (1899), 55-67; Fagnanus, lib. III, *de institutionibus*, c. 1, nn. 41-43.

[22] S. C. Ep. et Reg., *Massilien.*, mense iun. 1701—Bizzarri, *op. cit.*, p. 336; *Bracarensi*, 27 aug. 1616—Ferraris, *op. cit.*, "Moniales," II, n. 48.

of the monastery, the practice was declared to be free from any form of simony and was defended by canonical writers.[23]

Soon after the canonical recognition of religious dowry in the latter part of the sixteenth century, the Holy See adopted the policy of requiring all nuns to pay a dowry on the occasion of their entrance into religion, and monasteries were forbidden to admit them without it.[24] A girl could not be admitted to the reception of the habit unless the entire dowry was first placed on actual deposit.[25]

The Sacred Congregation of Bishops and Regulars, having observed that monasteries of nuns could not long be maintained without the help of a dowry from the new members, ordered, with papal approval, that dotal alms be paid by numerary nuns even though, according to the prescription of the Council of Trent, the number had been fixed according to the measure of the monastery's income.[26]

---

[23] Cf. *supra,* p. 14.

[24] Decr. S. C. Ep. et Reg., 20 mart. 1594: "Moniales velatae absque dote non debent admitti . . ."—Ferraris, "Moniales," II, n. 18; a similar decree was issued by the same Congregation in 1605: "Moniales velatae tam intra quam supra numerum absque dotali eleemosyna nequaquam admittantur."— Petra, *Commentaria,* III, const. XII, Innocentii IV (*Solet annuere*), sect. I, n. 28.

[25] S. C. Ep. et Reg., *Portugallien.,* 6 iun. 1605—Bizzarri, *Coll. S. C. Ep. et Reg.,* p. 334; Thomassinus quotes the following undated decree of the Sacred Congregation of the Council as found in the *Bibliotheca Praemonstratensi,* p. 356: "Non vestiantur moniales nec admittantur ad habitum, nisi prius parentes, vel ille, ad quos earum cura spectat, promptam habuerint pecuniam pro dote, vel eleemosyna consueta, et illam deposuerint solvendam monasterio post emissam professionem. . . . Hae eleemosynae, sive dotes, ante emissam professionem non solvantur monasterio, nec aliqua obligatio, aut renuntiatio fiat, nisi iuxta formam concilii."—pars III, lib. I, c. 54, n. 7.

[26] S. Congregatio super negotiis Episcoporum et Regularium quae animadvertens sanctimonialium monasteria sine dotium subsidio diu sustineri non posse, et propter ingruentes necessitates et casus inopinatos plerumque ad inopiam redigi, summis pontificibus approbantibus, prudenter sanxit ut dotales eleemosynae a monialibus numerariis persolverentur, tametsi numerus esset taxatus ad mensuram reddituum monasterii."—Fagnanus, lib. III, *de institutionibus,* c. 1, n. 24; Fagnanus does not mention the date of this document.

These declarations of the Sacred Congregation were important in the early canonical legislation on dowry. Previously it had been generally admitted as lawful for a poor monastery to demand money for the support of the members received.[27] But these pronouncements of the Sacred Congregation made no distinction as to the financial condition of the monastery. They approved the demanding of a dowry in *all* monasteries of women indiscriminately. Experience had shown that some monasteries which abounded in wealth had, in the course of time, been reduced to a condition of poverty. In practice, then, all monasteries of women were considered as having a just claim to a dowry from the new members.[28]

In spite of these expressions of the Holy See some bishops and monasteries were slow to divorce the idea of demanding a dowry from the concept of simony. In reply to questions submitted the Sacred Congregation of the Council stated expressly on two occasions that to demand and to receive a dowry in monasteries of women was free from any stain of simony.[29] These responses made no distinction as to the material resources of the monastery. Therefore they were considered as applicable to wealthy monasteries as well as to those pressed by poverty.[30]

Some authors held that it was simoniacal for a monastery to demand a dowry if the resources of the institution were sufficient to provide for the support of the members received. Suarez (1548-1617) said that a monastery which had sufficient income was bound to receive new candidates free and did not have the right to exact a price for their support. He stated that in such monasteries no custom to the contrary could be approved.[31]

---

[27] Cf. *supra*, p. 14.

[28] "De la dot des religieuses,"—*AJP*, IV (1860), p. 1527, n. 7; Cabassutius, *Theoria et Praxis Juris Canonici*, lib. V, c. V, n. 13.

[29] S. C. C., Belgii, 18 sept. 1683—*Fontes*, n. 2875; 14 apr. 1725—*Thesaurus Resolutionum* S. C. C., tom. III, 228; cf. Benedict XIV, *De Synodo Dioecesana*, lib. XI, c. 6, n. 1.

[30] Pennacchi, *Commentaria*, tom. I, appendix XXIV, 916; Benedict XIV, *op. cit.*, lib. XI, c. 6, n. 1; Schmalzgrueber, *Ius Ecclesiasticum Universum* (Romae, 1843-1845), tom. V, pars I, tit. III, n. 196.

[31] *De Virtute et Statu Religionis*, tract. III, lib. IV, c. 17, nn. 9-10.

Reiffenstuel (1641-1703) defended the right of a poor monastery to demand a dowry, but condemned the custom in rich institutes. He said that if, in the latter, a dowry was exacted under the title of support it was a false pretext, and the money was actually paid as a price of admission to the religious state. Those who took part in such transactions, he said, were guilty of simony in defiance of the divine law, and no custom to the contrary could ever be approved.[32]

Pirhing (1608-1679) stated that for a wealthy monastery to demand a price for the support of those entering it as members appeared to be simony as opposed to ecclesiastical law. Nevertheless, this author added that the contrary custom in monasteries of nuns should not be condemned, because the dowry was not exacted as an exchange of a spiritual for a temporal thing. It was exacted, rather, as a means for the support of the members in order that the monastery be not overburdened upon the reception of new persons, and in order that more members could be received than would otherwise be possible.[33]

Bouix (1808-1870) referred to a declaration of the Sacred Congregation of Bishops and Regulars issued on March 20, 1594, which stated that nuns must not be received without a dowry.[34] He did not believe that this regulation applied if the monastery was exceedingly rich and the candidate who was otherwise suitable was unable to pay the amount. He admitted that even wealthy monasteries could accept a dowry if it was offered voluntarily, but he denied that it was lawful for such a monastery to demand a dowry, and much less was the monastery obliged to demand it.[35]

The attitude of the Sacred Congregation of Bishops and Regulars appeared generally to require even wealthy monasteries to exact a dowry, notwithstanding the distinctions made and the views held by the above mentioned authors.

In a study of the legislation on religious dowry due allowance must be made for special circumstances and varying customs legiti-

---

[32] *Ius Canonicum Universum*, lib. V, tit. 3, nn. 163-176.
[33] *Ius Canonicum* (Dilingae, 1674-1678), lib. V, tit. III, sect. III, n. 59
[34] *Supra*, p. 22.
[35] *Tractatus de Jure Regularium*, tom. I, pars IV, sect. III, c. III, qq. 3-4.

mately established in different places. This is the principal explanation for the apparently conflicting responses issued by the Sacred Congregation of Bishops and Regulars concerning the time at which the dowry should be paid. For example, several decrees of this Congregation required the payment and actual deposit of the dowry *before* the girl was admitted to the reception of the habit.[36] Another decree stated that the profession of a novice could be postponed if the dowry had not yet been paid.[37] And, finally, the same Congregation in 1653 issued a response which permitted admission to profession *before* the payment of the dowry.[38] As Bouix remarks, these variations in practice and other similar departures from the fixed general norms must be attributed ·to local customs and conditions.[39]

Lay nuns (*conversae*) came under the same general rule as the choir nuns in the matter of dowry except that the amount required was smaller. Furthermore, the amount and necessity of the dowry for the lay nuns was determined more by the needs of the monastery than by any fixed rule. In fact, they could be received without a dowry if their services were needed by the monastery,[40] although in practice an indult was usually obtained.[41]

An important constitution, *"Ci è stato,"* dealing with the question of religious dowry was issued by Clement XIII (1758-1769) to the Vicar of Rome February 13, 1759.[42] This document was occasioned by abuses which had become prevalent in monasteries in the vicariate of Rome. Girls were admitted to the novitiate before they had made the deposit of their dowry. The result was that the order of the novitiate was often disturbed by the efforts

---

[36] Cf. *supra,* p. 22; Ferraris, "Moniales," II, n. 20.

[37] S. C. Ep. et Reg., 31 maii 1597—Ferraris, "Moniales," II, n. 25.

[38] S. C. Ep. et Reg., *Nucerina,* 14 febr. 1653—Ferraris, *loc. cit.*

[39] *Tractatus de Jure Regularium,* tom. I, pars IV, sect. III, c. III, q. 6.

[40] S. C. Ep. et Reg., 20 mart. 1594—Ferraris, *ibid.,* n. 18; Pellizzarius, *De Monialibus,* c. III, sect. II, n. 46; Petra, *Commentaria,* III const. XII, Innocentii IV (*Solet annuere*), sect. I, n. 54.

[41] Lucidi, *De Visitatione Sacrorum Liminum* (3. ed., Romae, 1883), vol. II, c. V, § 5, n. 186 (hereafter this work will be cited as *De Visitatione*); Goyeneche, "Consultationes,"—*CpRM,* XI (1930), 37.

[42] Bizzarri, *Coll. S. C. Ep. et Reg.,* p. 34-35.

of these novices to procure their dowry before the end of the year of probation. Furthermore, it often happened that they failed to have the money at the required time, and for that reason their profession had to be postponed. To remedy these abuses, Clement XIII restated in substance the response given a century and a half before by the Sacred Congregation of Bishops and Regulars to Portugal.[43] He ordered that no girl be admitted to the reception of the religious habit if she had not first deposited in the *Banco di S. Spirito* or a *Monte di Pietà* the entire amount of the dowry required by the constitutions of the monastery in which she wished to become a member. The superioress was forbidden to convoke the chapter for the vesting of a novice if the entire deposit had not been made. An authentic document attesting the fact of the effected deposit was ordered to be read in the chapter. Violation of this constitution by a superioress was punished by suspension from office *ipso facto,* and reinstatement could come only from the Supreme Pontiff.

The similarity between this constitution and the responses given by the Sacred Congregation of Bishops and Regulars within the first few years after the canonical recognition of dowry in the latter part of the sixteenth century shows a consistent policy of the Holy See in its dotal legislation, due allowance being made for particular customs.[44]

The constitution *"Ci è stato,"* written for the vicariate of Rome, was extended February 21, 1759, to apply to all monasteries in the papal states.[45] It gave a clear idea of the mind of the Holy See and re-established a norm for the guidance of the Sacred Congregations in rendering decisions. This constitution of Clement XIII was taken as a basis for the dowry legislation in the Code of Canon Law for monasteries of nuns.[46]

---

[43] Decr. S. C. Ep. et Reg., 6 iun. 1605—Bizzarri, *op. cit.,* p. 334.

[44] Cf. S. C. Ep. et Reg., *Camerinen.,* 2 dec. 1575—*Fontes,* n. 1320; *Civitatis Pennen.,* 8 febr. 1577—*Fontes,* n. 1327; 20 mart. 1594—Ferraris, "Moniales," II, n. 18; 20 maii 1596—Pellizzarius, *De Monialibus,* c. III, sect. II, n. 46; *Portugallien.,* 6 iun. 1605—Bizzarri, *Coll. S. C. Ep. et Reg.,* p. 334.

[45] Decr. S. C. Ep. et Reg., 21 febr. 1759—Bizzarri, *op. cit.,* p. 34; cf. Lucidi, *De Visitatione,* vol. II, c. 5, § 5, n. 188.

[46] Battandier, *Guide canonique,* p. 140.

ARTICLE IV. DEPOSIT OF THE DOWRY

A response from the Holy See in 1575 set forth the same regulations for the deposit of the dowry as had been prescribed by St. Charles Borromeo ten years before.[47] The dowry had to be deposited at the beginning of the novitiate in a bank or with a truly reliable person. At the time of the profession of the novice the depositary was required to transfer the money to the monastery.[48] Subsequent responses contained similar provisions and added that no one of the relatives of the novice was permitted to act as the depositary of her dowry.[49] Instances had arisen wherein relatives with whom the dowry of a novice had been deposited refused to pay the money to the monastery as specified.[50]

The ordinary was forbidden to make a law compelling the novices to deposit the dowry with him.[51] Nor could the money be paid by a novice directly to the monastery with the understanding that at the time of her profession it be used to constitute her dowry. If this rule was not observed then both the novice and the superioress who accepted the money could be punished for violation of the law of the Council of Trent.[52]

The Holy See was not satisfied with a fictitious or promised

---

[47] Cf. *supra*, p. 17.

[48] S. C. Ep. et Reg., *Camerinen.*, 2 dec. 1575—*Fontes*, n. 1320.

[49] S. C. Ep. et Reg., *Camerinen.*, 15 mart. 1594—Ferraris, "Moniales," II, n. 20; *Neapolitana*, 11 maii 1640, 10 ian. 1643, and 20 ian. 1645—Ferraris, *loc. cit.*; *Portugallien.*, 6 iun. 1605—Bizzarri, *op. cit.*, p. 334.

[50] Cf. S. C. Ep. et Reg., *Lucana*, 12 febr. 1597—*Fontes*, n. 1565.

[51] S. C. Ep. et Reg., *Vercellen.*, 15 nov. 1606—Lucidi, *De Visitatione*, Vol. II, c. V, § 5, n. 189.

[52] ". . . quin potius praecipit sancta Synodus sub anathematis poena dantibus, et recipientibus, ne hoc ullo modo fiat; et ut abeuntibus ante professionem omnia restituantur, quae sua erant: quod ut recte fiat, episcopus, etiam per censuras ecclesiasticas, si opus fuerit, compellat."— Conc. Trident., sessio XXV, *de regularibus et monialibus*, c. 16; the penalty "*sub anathematis poena*" of this law was interpreted as a *ferendae sententiae* penalty—cf. Pellizzarius, *De Monialibus*, c. III, sect. II, n. 57; cf. also S. C. Ep. et Reg., *Camerinen*, 1580—Barbosa, *Iuris Ecclesiastici Universi Libri Tres*, lib. I, c. 44, n. 37; S. C. C. *Meliten.*, 1590—Pallottini, *Collectio Omnium Conciliorum et Resolutionum apud Sacram Congregationem Cardinalium S. Concilii Tridentini Interpretum*, "Monasteria Monialium," § III, n. 51; Fagnanus, lib. III, *de regularibus*, c. 23, nn. 51-53.

deposit, but insisted on an actual and effective deposit of the dowry before the girl could be admitted to the reception of the habit.[53] In accepting the money the depositary was required to give assurance that at the time of the profession of the girl he would deliver the money to the monastery.[54] If he failed he could be compelled to abide by his agreement.[55]

The lack of observance of the decrees prescribed for the deposit of the dowry was strongly condemned by Clement XIII in his constitution *"Ci è stato."* This Pontiff insisted that the deposit of the dowry had to be made before the girl was to be admitted to the novitiate.[56]

The Congregation of Bishops and Regulars issued a decree *"Perpensis,"* May 3, 1902,[57] in which the prescriptions given to religious orders of men in the Encyclical *"Neminem latet,"* issued March 19, 1857, by Pius IX,[58] and the constitution *"Ad Universalis,"* issued February 7, 1862, by the same Pontiff,[59] were extended to apply to all orders of women of solemn vows. By virtue of the decree *"Perpensis,"* the novices were not admitted to solemn profession immediately after the completion of the novitiate, as had been the case formerly. In an effort to prevent the reception of unworthy candidates the novices were required to pass a three-year period in simple vows before being permitted to make solemn profession. Article 10 of the decree stated that the dowry prescribed in each monastery had to be paid to the monastery before the profession of simple vows.[60]

---

[53] S. C. Ep. et Reg., *Portugallien.*, 6 iun. 1605—Bizzarri, *op. cit.*, p. 334; *Portugallien.*, 6 iul. 1615, and *Brundusina*, 15 ian. 1616—Ferraris, *ibid.*, n. 23; *Panormitana*, 1617—*Fontes*, n. 1683; *Derthonen.*, 28 apr. 1645—*Fontes*, n. 1773.

[54] S. C. Ep. et Reg., *Camerinen.*, 15 mart. 1594—Barbosa, *op. cit.*, lib. I, c. 44, n. 36.

[55] S. C. Ep. et Reg., *Asculana*, 19 ian. 1630—Lucidi, *De Visitatione*, vol. II, c. V, § 5, n. 190.

[56] Cf. *supra*, p. 26.

[57] *Fontes*, n. 2039.

[58] Bizzarri, *op. cit.*, p. 853.

[59] *Fontes*, n. 532.

[60] "Dos pro quolibet monasterio statuta trandenda est ipsi monasterio ante professionem votorum simplicium."

Article 12 provided that for the dismissal of one in simple profession there was required in each case a recourse to the Holy See, in which recourse the grave causes that prompted or demanded such dismissal were to be listed and explained. And article 13 insisted that to anyone leaving during the term of her simple profession, either in view of a papal dispensation from her vows or because of an effected dismissal, there had to be restored the entire capital sum of the dowry, exclusive of its accrued fruits and revenues. However, the Congregation of Bishops and Regulars declared on March 26, 1904, that if a member died before the completion of the required three years of simple profession, the dowry should remain with the monastery, and was not to be returned to the relatives or heirs.[61]

ARTICLE V. QUANTITY OF THE DOWRY

The principal purpose of religious dowry is to provide the monastery with a stable source of income with which to supply the material necessities of the nuns. Therefore a major factor in arriving at an appraisal of the precise amount of dowry to be asked from aspirants to a particular monastery is the cost of maintenance and support. Naturally, this is a variable factor dependent upon many circumstances. For this reason the Holy See has refrained from specifying a definite sum applicable in all monasteries.[62] A minimum amount, however, was indicated in several responses issued in the first half of the seventeenth century. The Congregation of Bishops and Regulars prescribed that the quantity of the dowry should not be less than 200 *scudi* of Roman money, unless the founder of the monastery had stated a lesser amount.[63]

---

[61] *Fontes*, n. 2046.

[62] Cf. Fagnanus, lib. III, *de institutionibus*, c. 1, nn. 21-23; Joannes De Luca, *Theatrum Veritatis et Justitiae* (Coloniae Agrippinae, 1706), tom. XI, *De Dote*, discursus XI, n. 5 (hereafter this work will be cited as *De Dote*); Rodericus, *Resolutiones Questionum Regularium*, resolutio LIV, n. 4; Petra, *Commentaria*, III, const. XII, Innocentii IV (*Solet annuere*), sect. I, n. 43; Lucidi, *De Visitatione*, vol. II, c. V, § 5, n. 191.

[63] S. C. Ep. et Reg., *Ferentina*, 12 sept. 1614, and *Forolivien.*, 1 sept. 1645—Ferraris, "Moniales," II, n. 27; *Reatina*, 2 apr. 1618—Ferraris, *ibid.*, n. 28; cf. Vermeersch, *De Religiosis Institutis et Personis*, tom. I, pars IV, sect. I, c. II, n. 181, ad 1.

In the beginning the right to fix the amount of the dowry pertained to the ecclesiastical superiors over the nuns, that is, to the ordinary and the regular superior. This was true at least in many places.[64] In arriving at their decision as to the amount of the dowry to be established, these superiors were guided by such factors as the local custom, the cost of living in the locality, the endowment of the monastery, and any other circumstances which would make a greater or lesser dowry advisable or necessary.[65] Once the amount was fixed for a particular monastery, it was uniform for all candidates without exception of persons. Otherwise the way would be open for fraudulent practices and simoniacal pacts.[66]

Originally, the ordinary possessed rather extensive powers with regard to establishing and changing the quantity of the dowry. In individual cases and for a just reason he was permitted to diminish it, even against the will of the nuns, provided the monastery was able financially to accept the girl with a smaller dowry.[67]

It was forbidden for the nuns of a monastery to condone or diminish the established dowry even in a particular case. Nor could the sum be increased unless in the judgment of the bishop it became necessary on account of the poverty of the monastery to raise the fixed amount which was to be exacted from all candidates.[68]

As early as 1645 it was ordered that the dowry could not be diminished without the permission of the Congregation of Bishops and Regulars.[69] Authors stated that the custom grew up almost

---

[64] Cf. Pellizzarius, *De Monialibus,* c. III, sect. II, n. 42; Rodericus, *op. cit.,* resolutio LIV, n. 4.

[65] Cf. Petra, *Commentaria,* III, const. XII, Innocentii IV (*Solet annuere*), sect. I, n. 43.

[66] Cf. Petra, *ibid.,* n. 45; Joannes De Luca, tom. XI, *De Dote,* discursus CLXVII, nn. 5, 34-35.

[67] Cf. Pellizzarius, *loc. cit.;* Rodericus, *loc. cit.*

[68] Cf. Joannes De Luca, *ibid.,* n. 35; Petra, *ibid.,* n. 44.

[69] S. C. Ep. et Reg., 1 dec. 1645: "Dotes hodie minui non possunt sine licentia Sacrae Congregationis Episcoporum et Regularium."—Ferraris, "Moniales," II, n. 32.

from the beginning for this Congregation to establish the amount.[70] If special circumstances made a larger or a smaller dowry than the established sum necessary or expedient in a particular case the Holy See granted permission for the exception. For example, permission could be obtained to diminish the dowry in the case of a girl who, by reason of her special qualifications, would be very useful to the monastery but who was unable to pay the full amount. On the other hand, if the reception of a particular person who, because of advanced age or poor health, imposed an unusual burden on the monastery, the Holy See would permit a larger dowry to be exacted.[71]

The general norm forbade the exaction of a larger dowry from strangers than from those who lived in the town or city in which the monastery was located.[72] Customs to the contrary, however, were tolerated in some places. For example, the local girls were sometimes admitted with a lesser dowry because their ancestors had been responsible for the foundation and endowment of the monastery.[73]

If a sum of money larger than that which had been established as the legitimate dowry was exacted the monastery was bound to restore the excess. For it was forbidden to demand any more than had been established as the dowry in a given monastery. The exaction of anything in excess of that amount was reputed as simony. This prohibition, however, did not forbid or restrict in any way the voluntary offerings made by the candidate in addition to the accustomed dowry.[74]

---

[70] Cf. Pellizzarius, *De Monialibus,* c. III, sect. II, n. 43; Bouix, *Tractatus De Jure Regularium,* vol. I, pars IV, sect. III, c. III, q. 5; Piatus, *Praelectiones Juris Regularis* (Tornaci, 1906), tom. I, pars II, c. I, q. 96; Bachofen, *Compendium Juris Regularium* (New York, 1903), p. 110-111; "De la dot des religieuses,"—*AJP,* IV (1860), p. 1527, nn. 8-14.

[71] Cf. "De la dot des religieuses,"—*AJP,* IV (1860), 1531-1534; Petra, *ibid.,* nn. 48-50.

[72] Cf. S. C. Ep. et Reg., 3 sept. 1603—Lucidi, *De Visitatione,* vol. II, c. V, § 5, n. 200; Pellizzarius, *ibid.,* n. 44.

[73] Joannes De Luca, tom. XI, *De Dote,* discursus CLXVII, n. 37; Petra, *ibid.,* n. 51.

[74] Cf. Pellizzarius, *ibid.,* n. 45; Rodericus, *ibid.,* n. 5.

ARTICLE VI.   QUALITY OF THE DOWRY

The Holy See prescribed that the dowry be paid in money and not in immovable goods or similar substitutes.[75] Following the declarations of the Sacred Congregation of Bishops and Regulars, authors commonly taught that the dowry had to be paid in a stipulated amount of money (*pecunia numerata*).[76] Any exception to this form of payment required the permission of the Congregation of Bishops and Regulars, which permission was granted whenever the circumstances strongly urged the substitution, provided however that the financial condition of the monastery did not suffer thereby.[77]

ARTICLE VII.   ADMINISTRATION OF THE DOWRY

Since the dowries paid to a monastery often represent a large aggregate sum of money, the proper handling of these funds is vital to the economic welfare of the institution. For this reason the Holy See has taken definite action to maintain a careful vigilance over the administration of dowries. The ancient discipline governing the use of the capital sum of the dowry was not always uniform, especially when the two different types of dowry—the numerary and the supernumerary—were taken into consideration. In general, the monasteries enjoyed a greater authority and freedom of administration over the numerary than over the supernumerary dowry. The early discipline was quite uniform in insisting that the supernumerary dowry be invested.[78] In excep-

---

[75] S. C. Ep. et Reg., *Camerin.*, 28 mart. 1588—Ferraris, "Moniales," II, n. 19; *Interamen*, 2 maii 1614—Ferraris, *loc. cit.*

[76] Cf. Joannes De Luca, tom. XI, *De Dote*, discursus 167, n. 31; Pellizzarius, *op. cit.*, c. III, sect. II, n. 60; Petra, *Commentaria, ibid.*, n. 60; Bouix, *Tractatus De Jure Regularium*, tom. I, pars IV, sect. III, c. III, q. 6; Vermeersch, *De Religiosis Institutis et Personis*, tom. I, pars IV, sect. I, c. II, n. 181; Piatus, *Praelectiones Juris Regularis*, tom. I, pars II, c. I, q. 96; "De la dot des religieuses,"—*AJP*, IV (1860), p. 1538, n. 46.

[77] Cf. S. C. Ep. et Reg., *Brictinorien.*, 30 maii 1766—*Fontes*, n. 1876; *Ventimilien.*, 18 jul. 1834—*Fontes*, n. 1904; "De la dot des religieuses,"—*AJP*, IV (1860), pp. 1538-1540, nn. 46-52.

[78] S. C. Ep. et Reg., *Castelana*, 25 iul. 1574—Ferraris, *ibid.*, n. 36; *Mediolan.*, 22 mart. 1602; *Lauretana*, 13 mart. 1603; *Parmen.*, 15 sept.

tional cases it was possible to obtain permission for spending part
of it, but the Sacred Congregation would not grant permission for
spending more than half the total amount, even for the most urgent
cases.[79]

Although there were some cases in which the monastery was
forbidden to spend the numerary dowry,[80] the discipline of the
Church at first allowed this type of dowry to be expended for the
utility of the monastery,[81] unless the house was recently erected,
in which case even the numerary dowry had to be invested.[82]

Without distinguishing between the two kinds of dowry, the
Sacred Congregation of the Council declared in 1665 that a dowry
could not be alienated without the permission of the Holy See.[83]
By the end of the eighteenth century a change in the former
discipline had taken place. At that time the firm and constant
rule of the Holy See required that all monastic dowries—numerary
as well as supernumerary—were to be placed in safe and stable
investments. This was declared in two letters issued by the Sacred
Congregation of Bishops and Regulars, the first on April 21,
1780, and the second on November 24 of the same year. The
second letter added that this rule was to be observed in all
monasteries.[84]

The Sacred Congregation in 1784 expressly condemned the
opinion of those who held that the numerary dowry could be
spent for the utility of the monastery. In its ruling the Congregation stated that all monastic dowries had to be invested in productive capital and were not to be employed for other uses without

---

1603; *Fulginaten.,* 14 nov. 1625—Ferraris, *loc. cit.;* cf. Petra, *ibid.,* nn. 57-58;
Pellizzarius, *ibid.,* n. 61.

[79] S. C. Ep. et Reg., *Brixien.,* 23 febr. 1603—Ferraris, *ibid.,* n. 42; *Perusina,*
13 ian. (year is not given)—Ferraris, *loc. cit.;* cf. Petra, *loc. cit.*

[80] S. C. Ep. et Reg., *Urbevetana,* 29 ian. 1601—*Fontes,* n. 1600.

[81] S. C. Ep. et Reg., *Ariminen.,* 22 maii 1601—Ferraris, *ibid.,* n. 29;
Ferrarien., 23 mart. 1601—Ferraris, *loc. cit.;* cf. Monacelli, *Formularium
Legale Practicum Fori Ecclesiastici,* pars II, tit. 13, form. 5, n. 3.

[82] S. C. Ep. et Reg., *Capacien.,* 23 iul. 1603—Lucidi, *De Visitatione,* vol.
II, c. V, § 5, n. 191; cf. Petra, *ibid.,* n. 58.

[83] S. C. C., *Olomucen.,* 11 iul. 1665—*Fontes,* n. 2795, ad 14.

[84] Cf. Lucidi, *De Visitatione,* vol. II, c. V, § 5, n. 191.

Apostolic permission.[85] It was forbidden for the monasteries to use the dotal funds for building projects or for the payment of debts.[86]

The newly established Sacred Congregation of Religious published on July 30, 1909, the instruction *"Inter Ea,"*[87] in which it reaffirmed the previous discipline of the Sacred Congregation of Bishops and Regulars by prohibiting the disposal of religious dowries. This instruction set forth the norms to be observed by all religious institutes in contracting debts and in alienating goods. Article 12 stated emphatically that under no condition should the dowry be spent during the lifetime of the respective nun or sister. The permission of the Holy See had to be sought if, on account of extremely grave circumstances, the alienation of even one dowry was judged necessary. The prohibition in this instruction extended only to the capital sum of the dowry. The interest and other revenue which had accrued from the investment of the capital could be consigned to the general treasury of the monastery. Article 14 stated that violators of the prescriptions of the decree should be gravely punished; and if the violation was concerning those things which by common law or by the present decree required Apostolic permission, the guilty incurred *ipso facto* the penalties inflicted on those who alienated ecclesiastical goods. Therefore, since article 12 required the permission of the Holy See to alienate the dowry, those who did so without this permission incurred *ipso facto* the penalty for alienating ecclesiastical goods. According to the constitution *"Apostolicae Sedis"* of Pius IX, October 12, 1869, those who alienated ecclesiastical goods without the permission of the Holy See incurred excommunication reserved to no one.[88]

---

[85] S. C. Ep. et Reg., *Firmana,* 18 iun. 1784—*Fontes,* n. 1880.

[86] S. C. Ep. et Reg., *Perugia,* 29 nov. 1779, "Discipline des Communautés," —*AJP,* XXIII (1884), p. 965, n. 37; "De la dot des religieuses,"—*AJP,* IV (1860), p. 1551, n. 82.

[87] *Fontes,* n. 4394.

[88] IV, ad 3—*Fontes,* n. 552.

ARTICLE VIII.   RESTITUTION OF THE DOWRY

Prior to the decree *"Perpensis,"* in 1902, solemn profession in religious institutes of women with solemn vows followed immediately after the completion of the novitiate.[89]   Although the candidate was required to deposit her dowry before entering the novitiate, the money was not delivered to, nor was it acquired by, the monastery until she made profession.   If for any reason she failed to be professed she recovered the dowry which had been deposited before she began the novitiate.[90]   In a case in which the profession of a candidate was invalid because it was made contrary to the form prescribed by the Council of Trent the Congregation of Bishops and Regulars declared that the dowry should be refunded to the father, allowing the monastery, however, to retain a part of it to cover the expenses incurred for the support of the girl while she was in the monastery.[91]

The Congregation of Bishops and Regulars declared in 1581 in two separate responses to the Bishop of Spoleto that if the candidate died during the year of probation the dowry should be restored to her relatives,[92] but if she died after profession the monastery had thereby acquired a right to the dowry and was entitled to keep it.[93]   The monastery did not acquire a right to the dowry of a deceased novice who, before the completion of the novitiate, made profession at the point of death.[94]

The Congregation of the Council in 1627 condemned as an intolerable abuse the practice of compelling the monastery to return, either in whole or in part, the dowry of a deceased nun.[95] The same Congregation declared in 1637 that nuns who were pro-

---

[89] Cf. *supra*, p. 28.

[90] Cf. S. C. Ep. et Reg., *Assisien.*, 14 nov. 1581—*Fontes*, n. 1392; *Reatina*, 19 iun. 1601—*Fontes*, n. 1604; S. C. C., *Eugubina*, 26 nov. 1650—*Fontes*, n. 2714; cf. Petra, *Commentaria*, III, Const. XII, Innocenti IV (*Solet annuere*), sect. II, nn. 47-48.

[91] S. C. Ep. et Reg., *Spoletana*, 11 nov. 1578—*Fontes*, n. 1344.

[92] S. C. Ep. et Reg., *Spoletana*, 14 febr. 1581—*Fontes*, n. 1383.

[93] S. C. Ep. et Reg., *Spoletana*, 18 iul. 1581—*Fontes*, n. 1386.

[94] S. C. C., *Ordinis Minorum S. Francisci*, 20 mart. 1649—*Fontes*, n. 2696.

[95] S. C. C., *Mutinen.*, 11 iun. 1627—Lucidi, *De Visitatione*, vol. II, c. V, § 5, n. 198.

fessed in one monastery and then wished with proper permission
to transfer to another monastery of stricter observance could not
take with them the dowry paid to the first monastery.[96]

A problem arose over the disposal of the dowry of a nun when
she left the monastery after solemn profession, or when she transferred to another religious institute. It was argued by some that
the dowry was accessory to the person of the nun in such a way
that it should be refunded to her or transferred with her; furthermore, that the monastery could not retain the dowry of a nun
who transferred to another institute, since with the completion of
the transfer the first monastery was relieved of the burden of
supporting her. Writers generally agreed, however, that the
dowry was acquired by the monastery at the time of solemn
profession, irrespective of whether the nun persevered in the
institute or not.[97] The fact that by the departure or transfer the
monastery was freed from the obligation of supporting the nun
did not alter the case. For the obligation of the monastery to
support the members arose, not from the dowry given, but rather
from the nature of the profession itself.[98]

In practice, controversies over the ownership of the dowry of
a nun who transferred to another institute were not frequent, since
the transfer was usually forbidden without the permission of the
Holy See.[99] In issuing individual rescripts granting permission
for a nun to transfer the Sacred Congregations included a clause
pertaining to the dowry based on the circumstances of the case
and the cause of the transfer. Ferraris ($+$ c. 1763), citing a
number of cases decided by the Sacred Congregation of Bishops
and Regulars from 1580 to 1635, concluded that a nun who

---

[96] S. C. C., decr. 27 iun. 1637—Pallottini, "Moniales," § II, n. 13.

[97] Joannes De Luca, tom. XI, *De Dote,* discursus 167, nn. 30-31; Pelliz-
zarius, *De Monialibus,* c. III, sect. II, nn. 69-70; Pignatelli, *Consultationes
Canonicae,* tom. I, consult. 432, nn. 1-13; Cajetanus, *Juris Canonici Universi
Commentarius* (Monachii, 1705), lib. III, tit. XXXI, c. VIII, nn. 46-49;
Rodericus, *Resolutiones Questionum Regularium,* resolutio LIV, n. 7; Petra,
Commentaria, III, const. XVI, Eugenii IV (*Regularem*), sect. I, nn. 12-16;
Goyeneche, "Consultationes,"—*CpRM,* V (1924), 390-393.

[98] Pignatelli, *ibid.,* n. 11.

[99] Petra, *ibid., n.* 15; Pellizzarius, *ibid.,* n. 70.

transferred to another monastery was obliged to leave her dowry in the first, and pay a new dowry to the second monastery unless the Sacred Congregation disposed otherwise.[100] If the transfer was voluntary on the part of the nun, or if it was just and necessary and was not occasioned by the monastery, then the Holy See in permitting the transfer was accustomed to demand that the dowry be left with the first monastery and a new dowry be paid to the second.[101] It was otherwise, however, when the transfer was occasioned by the fault of the monastery itself, for in this case the Sacred Congregation demanded that the first monastery surrender the dowry to the monastery to which the nun transferred.[102]

Monacelli, a contemporary of Ferraris, enumerated seven typical cases decided by the Holy See from 1615 to 1705. Basing his conclusion on the solution of these cases, he taught that the dotal alms paid on the occasion of entrance into a monastery were at the time of profession acquired irrevocably by that monastery, and were never refunded to a nun who transferred to another institute, unless the Supreme Pontiff or the Sacred Congregation ordered it.[103]

Even though not required to return the dowry, the first monastery was sometimes obliged by the Holy See to make a contribution to help the nun raise a new dowry to be paid to the second monastery.[104]

The jurisprudence of the Congregation of Bishops and Regulars showed an increasing tendency in favor of the restoration of the dowry to a nun who left the monastery.[105] In regard to sisters in simple vows, the policy was to return the dowry if for any

---

[100] Ferraris, "Moniales," II, n. 50.
[101] Monacelli, *Formularium Legale Practicum Fori Ecclesiastici,* pars II, tit. XIII, form. V, nn. 21-22; Petra, *Commentaria,* III, const. XVI, Eugenii IV (*Regularem*), sect. I, nn. 15-16; Joannes De Luca, tom. XI, *De Dote,* discursus 167, n. 28.
[102] S. C. Ep. et Reg., *Ferrarien.,* 17 febr. 1702—Monacelli, *ibid.,* n. 21; Petra, *ibid.,* n. 16.
[103] *Ibid.,* nn. 21-22.
[104] S. C. Ep. et Reg., *Valentina,* 13 febr. 1699—Petra, *ibid.,* n. 16.
[105] Goyeneche, "Consultationes,"—*CpRM,* V (1924), 391-392.

reason she left the convent.[106]   An application of this policy is
found in the decree *"Perpensis,"* issued by the Sacred Congregation of Bishops and Regulars on May 3, 1902, which required that
all candidates for religious institutes of women with solemn vows
had to be professed in simple vows for three years before making
solemn profession.   Article 13 stated that if one of these sisters
in simple vows left the monastery, either in virtue of a dispensation from her vows granted by the Holy See, or because of a
decree of dismissal, her entire dowry, less the interest, should be
returned to her.[107]

Authors writing near the beginning of the twentieth century
still held that the dowry was acquired by the monastery upon the
solemn profession of a nun, but said that equity demanded restoration in certain cases.   Vermeersch (1858-1936) stated that the
Sacred Congregation was accustomed to prescribe the restoration
of the dowry to a nun in solemn vows: a) if the monastery gave
cause for the departure; b) if the nun transferred to another religious institute; c) if the nun was without means of support; in
this case the monastery was obliged either to restore the dowry
or to provide for her maintenance.[108]   Piat (1815-1904) said that
if the cause of the departure was just and necessary and was not
occasioned by the monastery, the monastery was not obliged to
return the dowry, nor to provide for the nun's support except to
help constitute a new dowry if she lacked the means; the monastery
could free itself from this obligation by returning the dowry.   As
had been held by previous authors, Piat added that if the monastery
had given cause for the departure, the Holy See was accustomed
to demand the restitution of the dowry.[109]

---

[106] Cf. S. C. C., *Civitatis Castellanae,* 3 mart. 1792—*Fontes,* n. 3875; cf.
Lucidi, *op. cit.,* vol. II, c. V, § 8, n. 445.

[107] *Fontes,* n. 2039.

[108] *De Religiosis Institutis et Personis,* tom. I, pars IV, sect. I, c. II, n. 181.

[109] *Praelectiones Juris Regularis,* tom. I, pars II, c. I, q. 96.

CHAPTER IV

Dowry for Religious Congregations Whose Members Took Simple Vows

ARTICLE I. PRIOR TO 1901

Besides the monasteries of women with solemn vows, there grew up in the Church another class of religious society, the distinguishing feature of which was the fact that the members took only simple vows, either perpetual or temporary. This type of institute is known as a religious congregation.[1] Full juridical approbation of religious institutes of simple vows came from the Holy See only after several centuries; first there was condemnation, then there came toleration, and finally approval.[2] The first general legislation pertaining to religious congregations of simple vows was contained in the constitution *"Conditae a Christo"* of Leo XIII, issued on December 8, 1900.[3]

With the rapid spread and multiplication of religious congregations in the nineteenth century the Holy See desired that they submit their constitutions for examination and approval. Even before specific regulations governing the formation of the constitutions of these congregations were furnished by the Holy See, the Sacred Congregation of Bishops and Regulars insisted on certain standards of discipline in a given set of constitutions before granting it approval. From the comments made by the Sacred Congregation on the various constitutions submitted for approbation a

---

[1] Canon 488, n. 2.

[2] Cf. Pius V, const. *"Circa Pastoralis,"* 29 maii 1566—*Fontes,* n. 112; Benedict XIV, const. *"Quamvis justo,"* 30 apr. 1749—*Fontes,* n. 398; Lucidi, *De Visitatione,* vol. II, c. V, § 8, nn. 263-265. For a detailed account of the growth of Religious Congregations see Orth, *The Approbation of Religious Institutes,* The Catholic University of America, Canon Law Studies, n. 71 (Washington, D. C.: The Catholic University of America, 1931), pp. 39-73.

[3] *Fontes,* n. 644.

clear idea can be gathered of the nature of the regulations which were necessary to be incorporated into the constitutions in order to merit the approval of the Holy See.

The dotal provisions of the newly approved constitutions of the religious congregations showed many similarities to the general dowry legislation of the Holy See. It must be noted, however, that the former legislation applied only to those religious institutes of women in which the members made solemn profession.[4]

In order to promote a condition of economic stability the Congregation of Bishops and Regulars desired that the constitutions contain provisions requiring the payment of a dowry by the candidates upon their entrance.[5]

In cases of necessity the Holy See granted exceptions to the general rule which obliged all institutes to require a dowry from the entrants. One example was the Little Sisters of the Poor. And in 1898 a general dispensation from the dowry was granted to the Little Sisters of the Assumption.[6] The demanding of an equal sum from each candidate became the law, and it destroyed the former abuse which sometimes required the surrender to the institute of all the candidate's possessions.[7] As in the legislation for solemn vow institutes the dowry was to be paid in a stipulated sum of money (*numerata pecunia*).[8]

---

[4] Cf. Bouix, *Tractatus De Jure Regularium*, tom. I, pars IV, sect. III, c. III, q. 7.

[5] S. C. Ep. et Reg., *Sorores S. Vincentii a Paulo Famulae Pauperum, Gandaven.*, 30 apr. 1860, n. 3: "Ut domus instituti aliquam dotationem habere possint fortasse expediret ut moderata dos investienda a profitendis solveretur."—Bizzarri, *Coll. S. C. Ep. et Reg.*, p. 778; Battandier, *Guide canonique* (Paris, 1898), p. 86, n. 94.

[6] Battandier, *Guide canonique* (1923), p. 141, n. 170.

[7] S. C. Ep. et Reg., *Sorores a S. Maria et Josepho, Lemovicen.*, 11 iul. 1860, n. 8: "Expediret ut dos pro omnibus aequalis constitueretur."— Bizzarri, *op. cit.*, p. 784; *Filles de la Charitè servantes des pauvres, Montreal*, 25 apr. 1860, n. 6: "Haud expedit ut omnia bona professarum vi constitutionum ad institutm transeant, sed potius determinata dos praefinienda est." —Battandier, *Guide canonique* (1898), p. 86, n. 94.

[8] S. C. Ep. et Reg., *Adoratrices SSmi. Sacramenti*, 1 sept. 1860, n. 6: "Iuxta decreta S. Congregationis, dotes persolvi debent in numerata pecunia." —Bizzarri, *op. cit.*, p. 788; Battandier, *Guide canonique* (1898), p. 88, n. 97.

The lay sisters (*conversae*) as well as the choir sisters were obliged to bring a dowry. And although the amount for the members of each group could differ, nevertheless all the sisters of the same rank were obliged to give an equal sum. Upon receiving the dowry, which was to be paid before profession, the institute was bound to place it in productive investments and was forbidden to alienate the capital sum during the lifetime of the respective sister. The accrued interest from the investments, however, became the immediate property of the institute and could be placed in the common treasury. If the religious departed or was dismissed from the institute her entire dowry, less the accrued interest, was to be restored to her. These provisions were contained in the comments of the Sacred Congregation of Bishops and Regulars to the Sisters of S. Aignan, Orleans.[9]

There was no uniform regulation in determining the amount of the dowry to be paid. The Holy See merely insisted on the necessity of this payment, leaving the determination of the quantity to the individual constitutions. If the Sacred Congregation considered the amount reasonable for the respective institute, then approval was given to the sum specified when general approbation was accorded to the constitutions.[10] After the quantity was fixed and approved, the Holy See reserved to itself the right to dispense from or to diminish it.[11] The Sacred Congregation did not approve the provisions in constitutions which reserved to the superioresses the right to admit candidates without a dowry, or with a

---

[9] S. C. Ep. et Reg., *Soeurs de S. Aignan, Orleans*, 3 sept. 1892, n. 6: "Afferant dotem spiritualem, sive sint choristae, sive sint conversae, sed unicuique proportionatam et aequaliter ab omnibus solvendam ante primam professionem, quae statuatur in fundo frugifero, nec alienari poterit quoad vixerit quia, salvis fructibus, restituenda erit ad quas pertinet quatenus ab instituto vel exierit, vel dimittetur."—Battandier, *Guide canonique* (1898), p. 87, n. 95; cf. also S. C. C., *Civitatis Castellanae,* 3 mart. 1792—*Fontes,* n. 3875; S. C. Ep. et Reg., *Comen.,* 1 dec. 1758—*Fontes,* n. 1874; "De la dot des religieuses,"—*AJP,* IV (1860), p. 1556, n. 94; Lucidi, *De Visitatione,* tom. II, c. V, § 8, n. 445; Vermeersch, *De Religiosis Institutis et Personis,* tom. I, pars IV, sect. I, c. II, n. 182.

[10] "De la dot des religieuses,"—*AJP,* IV (1860), p. 1558, n. 98; Battandier, *Guide canonique* (1898), p. 87, n. 96; Vermeersch, *loc. cit.;* Bastien, *Directoire canonique* (Abbaye de Maredsous, 1904), n. 109.

[11] "De la dot des religieuses,"—*loc. cit.*

lesser amount than that which was prescribed.[12]   Rather than concede to the superioresses the faculty of dispensing from or diminishing the dowry, the Congregation advised that a smaller dowry be prescribed in general, which would thereby lessen the frequency of the need of a dispensation or diminution.[13]

Previous to the time of Pius IX (1846-1878) it was disputed whether or not legacies left by pious benefactors to be used to constitute the dowry of girls who wished to embrace the religious life could be applied to candidates for admission into institutes where only simple vows were taken.   The question was settled by a decree of the Congregation of Bishops and Regulars on November 12, 1847, in which it was stated that such legacies could be used for institutes of simple vows provided the following conditions were fulfilled: 1) that the institute had been approved by the Holy See; 2) that the simple vows were perpetual; 3) that the testator had not specified expressly that the funds were to be given only to those candidates who wished to enter monasteries where solemn vows were taken.[14]

ARTICLE II.   THE *Normae* OF 1901

After the promulgation of the constitution *"Conditae a Christo,"* which fixed the broad outline of canonical legislation for congregations of simple vows, the Sacred Congregation of Bishops and Regulars issued a code of three hundred and twenty-five articles to serve as a guide in the practical formation of constitutions.   This instruction is known as the *"Normae"* of 1901.[15]

---

[12] S. C. Ep. et Reg., *Sorores Charitatis Filiarum Immaculatae Conceptionis, Paderbonensis,* 10 mart. 1860, n. 9: "Nimis ampla videtur facultas, quae conceditur moderatrici recipiendi novitias sine dote, quod quamdam alienationis speciem praesefert."—Bizzarri, *Coll. S. C. Ep. et Reg.,* p. 777.

[13] S. C. Ep. et Reg., *Sorores a Presentatione B. M. V., Albiensis,* 23 iul. 1860, n. 8: "Periculosa videtur facultas imminuendi dotes, vel ab eis dispensandi, quae conceditur moderatrici generali.   Fortasse magis expediret ut minor dos in genere praescriberetur."—Bizzarri, *op. cit.,* p. 786.

[14] S. C. Ep. et Reg., 12 nov. 1847—Bizzarri, *op. cit.,* p. 120.

[15] *Normae Secundum Quas S. Congr. Episcoporum et Regularium Procedere Solet in Approbandis Novis Institutis Votorum Simplicium* (Romae, 1901).

The dotal norms, embracing articles 91 to 95 inclusive, consisted of a codification of the discipline which had been followed in this matter by the Sacred Congregation in approving constitutions submitted previous to the publication of the *"Normae."*

Article 91 stated that every institute of sisters of simple vows must fix the quantity of dowry to be paid by the entrants. An equal amount should be required from all sisters of the same rank. The standard sum, however, for the lay sisters should be lower than that for the choir sisters.[16]

Article 92 reserved to the Congregation of Bishops and Regulars all power of dispensing from or lessening the established dowry. Therefore, neither the religious superioress nor the ordinary could, without special authorization from the Holy See, remit the dowry, either in whole or in part.[17]

Article 93 pertained to the payment of the dowry. This article required in the first place that the dowry was to be made secure for the institute by a reliable guaranty, which was to be done before the investing with the religious habit; and in the second place that the dowry was to be delivered to the institute immediately before the profession.[18]

Article 94 forbade the alienation of the dowry. Upon its payment to the institute the dowry had to be placed in a lawful, safe, and productive investment.[19]

Finally, article 95 gave the norm for establishing the ultimate dominion of the dowry. If a sister left the convent or was dismissed, then the capital sum of her dowry had to be returned to her. The interest, however, which the investment earned during the time she remained in the convent was acquired by the

---

[16] "Quodlibet Institutum Sororum praefigere debet dotem solvendam, aequalem, pro sororibus chori; et etiam pro sororibus conversis seu coadiutricibus dotem quidem minorem, sed pro harum singulis aequalem."

[17] "Statutam dotem moderatrix non potest remittere neque imminuere sine licentia Sacrae Congregationis."

[18] "Statuta dos tuta reddatur favore instituti per solidam cautionem, antequam candidata habitu induatur; tradenda est autem instituto proxime ante professionem."

[19] "Tradita dos alienari non potest, sed probe, tuto ac fructuose collocari debet."

institute.[20]   It was only upon the death of the sister that the capital of her dowry was acquired irrevocably by the religious congregation.

The prohibition of alienating the dowry, as stated in article 94 of the *"Normae,"* was reaffirmed and emphasized in the instruction *"Inter Ea"* of the Sacred Congregation of Religious on July 30, 1909.[21]   This instruction was directed to *all* religious institutes, whether of solemn or of simple vows.   Article 12 called attention to the previous legislative enactments against the alienation of dowries and ordered strict adherence to that legislation.   Under no condition was it permitted to spend the dowry while the respective nun or sister was living.   The practical reason for this provision was self-evident, especially in congregations of simple vows, since the sister had a right to recover her dowry if she left the institute or was dismissed.   If, in view of very grave and serious reasons, it was judged necessary to alienate even one dowry, the permission of the Holy See had to be obtained.[22]

---

[20] "Si aliqua soror ab instituto discedat vel dimittatur, dos sua ipsi, sine fructibus tamen, restituatur."

[21] *Fontes,* n. 4394.

[22] Cf. *supra,* p. 34.

HISTORICAL SUMMARY

In most of the early monastic rules prospective candidates were permitted, in disposing of their worldly goods, to bestow some or all of these goods on the monastery. None of the early rules, however, imposed such contributions as obligatory or as a condition of entrance.

With the growth and spread of the religious life some unscrupulous and avaricious religious superiors and superioresses took advantage of their position to acquire financial gain by demanding a price from candidates who sought admission. The II General Council of Nice (787) sharply condemned the practice and subjected the guilty to severe penalties. The Council stated explicitly, however, that voluntary offerings made by the candidate or her parents were permitted and could be accepted by the monastery.

The laws of the Council of Nice against simony in connection with entrance into religion were re-enacted in substance over and over again during the middle ages in both particular and general legislation. The IV General Council of the Lateran (1215) was especially vigorous in its condemnation of the abuse whereby monasteries of women demanded a price from the candidates.

Not until shortly after the Council of Trent was the exaction of a dowry from women entering religion recognized and admitted as lawful. St. Charles Borromeo, in the I and II Provincial Councils of Milan, in 1565 and 1569 respectively, is recognized as offering the first instance of a law that exacted a dowry from candidates for the religious life. The practice soon received the recognition and approval of the Holy See through responses given by the Sacred Congregation of Bishops and Regulars. Thus the Holy See, allowing the custom to be introduced into monasteries, controlled and developed it through legislation.

The Holy See adopted the general policy of requiring the payment of a dowry by all women entering the religious life.

Specific regulations were issued governing the payment, the nature, and the amount of the dowry, as well as its proper administration and ultimate ownership. That legislation applied only to religious institutes of women in which solemn vows were taken. Eventually, however, after having first condemned and then tolerated religious congregations of simple vows, the Holy See placed its full stamp of approval on this type of religious institute and applied to them many of the principles of the previous dotal legislation.

Through its approval and regulation of the religious dowry the Holy See manifests a solicitude for the welfare and progress of the religious life among women. The income received from the dowries serves to promote and perpetuate the particular pious or charitable work to which the members of each institute have consecrated their lives.

PART II

CANONICAL COMMENTARY

CHAPTER V

NECESSITY OF THE PAYMENT OF A DOWRY

Prior to the Code the legislation of the Holy See relative to the dowry for monasteries of women with solemn vows was entirely distinct from that for religious congregations of women with simple vows. For example, the *Normae* of 1901, containing five articles on dowry, applied only to the latter type of religious institute. On the other hand, most of the dotal legislation in the Code applies equally to all institutes of women religious without any distinction as to the solemnity or perpetuity of the vows. There are a few exceptions to this rule, however, one of which concerns the obligation of demanding a dowry from the candidates. Consequently, the present chapter on the necessity of the dowry considers first the law for monasteries of women with solemn vows and then the law for congregations of women with simple vows.

ARTICLE I. MONASTERIES OF NUNS WITH SOLEMN VOWS

Canon 547, § 1: In monasteriis monialium postulans afferat dotem in constitutionibus statutam aut legitima consuetudine determinatam.

Canon 547, § 1, demands the payment of a dowry by postulants seeking to become members of a monastery of nuns. Although the determination of the amount is left to the particular constitutions or to legitimate custom, the obligation of a dowry is imposed by the common law on all monasteries of nuns.[1] The law applies directly to monasteries in which the members actually have solemn vows and seems likewise to extend to those institutes whose vows are solemn, but whose members in some places, by order of the Holy See, take simple vows. Canon 488, n. 7, states that these latter are included in the term *moniales,* unless from the nature of the case or from the context of the law it is evident that only those nuns are meant who actually have taken solemn vows. Therefore, the presumption is in favor of the extension to these religious of the laws affecting monasteries of nuns, and it may be said that it is only by way of exception that they are excluded from the term *moniales* in the Code. It is not evident from the nature of the case or from the context that they should be excluded from the law of canon 547, § 1. Furthermore, the wording of paragraph three of the same canon, which speaks of the dowry in "societies of simple vows," does not seem to include them, for strictly considered they are not "societies of simple vows," but rather societies of solemn vows although the members in some places by order of the Holy See take only simple vows. Therefore, it seems more correct to include this type of religious in paragraph one of canon 547 and affirm that they are obliged by the common law to require a dowry.[2]

Since the Code, in prescribing the obligation of a dowry in monasteries of nuns, makes no distinction between the different classes of members, that is, between the choir nuns and the lay nuns, the law must be considered as applicable to both.[3] In

---

[1] Cf. Vromant, *De Bonis Ecclesiae Temporalibus,* p. 267, n. 252, 1); Coronata, *Institutiones,* I, p. 724, n. 577; Vermeersch-Creusen, *Epitome,* I, p. 497, n. 698; Wernz-Vidal, *De Religiosis,* p. 222, n. 268.

[2] Cf. Blat, *Commentarium Textus Codicis Iuris Canonici,* vol. II, *Ius De Religiosis Et Laicis* (3. ed., Romae: Apud Angelicum, 1938), p. 312, n. 325; Coronata, *Institutiones,* I, p. 724, footnote 8; Larraona, "Commentarium Codicis,"—*CpRM,* XX (1939), 80-81. The opposite opinion is held by Toso, *Ad Codicem Iuris Canonici Commentaria Minora,* tom. II, pars II (Romae: Jus Pontificium, 1927), p. 108, n. 2 (hereafter this work will be cited as *Commentaria*).

[3] Cf. Goyeneche, "Consultationes,"—*CpRM,* XI (1930), 37; Schaefer, *De Religiosis,* p. 502, n. 228; Vromant, *De Bonis Ecclesiae Temporalibus,* p. 268, n. 252.

regard to the amount, however, the constitutions or custom of the institute are free to require, as they frequently did in the old law, a lesser dowry from the lay nuns.

In virtue of canon 5 an immemorial custom of admitting lay nuns without a dowry may be permitted to continue if the ordinary decides that it cannot prudently be abolished because of special circumstances.[4]

Special provisions were made by the Holy See for the reception without a dowry of extern sisters into monasteries of nuns with solemn vows. This class of sisters, bound by the same rule as the nuns in the monastery, and subject to the same superioress, was introduced for the purpose of conducting the external affairs of the community. Special permission of the Holy See is required in each case to establish this class of religious. Their vows are simple, and they are not bound by the strict law of the cloister which obliges the ordinary or intern members. In order to safeguard the religious life of the extern sisters the Sacred Congregation of Religious, with the approval of the Holy Father, published on July 16, 1931, a special list of statutes to be adopted and observed by these sisters, no matter to what order they may belong. Article 51 forbids the exaction of a dowry, but states that the extern sisters should bring clothing and other furnishings according to the norms prescribed by the superioress of the monastery.[5] Cardinal La Puma, who was secretary of the Sacred Congregation of Religious at the time the statutes were published, in commenting on article 51, states that a dowry must not be exacted from the extern sisters, nor should it even be mentioned, lest it lead to a double category of religious within this class. He added, however, that if an extern sister brought something after the manner of a dowry, the rules governing dowry were to be observed. Although the statutes forbid the exaction of a dowry, he said, they do not forbid the acceptance of it if offered.[6]

---

[4] Blat, *Commentarium,* II, p. 313, n. 327; Wernz-Vidal, *De Religiosis,* p. 223, n. 268; Vermeersch-Creusen, *Epitome,* I, p. 497, n. 698; Goyeneche, *loc. cit.;* Larraona, *ibid.,* p. 82.

[5] "Statuta a Sororibus Externis Monasteriorum Monialium Cuiusque Ordinis Servanda,"—*CpRM,* XIV (1933), 167.

[6] Cf. *CpRM, loc. cit.*

ARTICLE II.   RELIGIOUS CONGREGATIONS OF SISTERS
WITH SIMPLE VOWS

Canon 547, § 3: In religionibus votorum simplicium, quod ad religiosarum dotem pertinet, standum constitutionibus.

Prior to the promulgation of the Code of Canon Law article 91 of the *Normae* of 1901 governed the necessity of a dowry in religious communities with simple vows.   This article prescribed that every institute of sisters with simple vows demand a dowry from all candidates.[7]   Canon 547, § 3, introduces a modification of that ruling by stating that the particular constitutions are to be followed with respect to the dowry.   In other words, the present common law does not require all such institutes to make the payment of a dowry obligatory, but rather leaves the determination of the necessity of a dowry to the individual constitutions. The constitutions, therefore, may or may not require a dowry; they may require it from all candidates indiscriminately, or only from the choir sisters; or they may require a lesser amount from the lay sisters than from the choir sisters.[8]

The freedom committed to the constitutions in this matter is not an unrestricted power, but is limited by such factors as the nature of the work and the purpose of the institute.   Final judgment rests with the Sacred Congregation of Religious to whom the constitutions of all religious congregations seeking pontifical approbation must be submitted for approval.   In diocesan congregations the local ordinary is the one who passes judgment. While a great diversity of regulations are found in the constitutions of the various religious congregations, the Sacred Congregation of Religious usually demands that at least a small

---

[7] Cf. *supra*, p. 43.

[8] Cf. Vermeersch-Creusen, *Epitome,* I, p. 497, n. 698; Toso, *Commentaria,* lib. II, pars II, p. 108, n. 4; Oesterle, *Praelectiones Iuris Canonici,* I (Romae 1931), 301; Wernz-Vidal, *De Religiosis,* p. 223, n. 268; Bastien, *Directoire canonique a l'usage des congrégations à voeux simples* (3. ed., Bruges: Charles Beyaert, 1923), p. 64, n. 99.

dowry be required.[9] Although a small dowry may not add materially to the income or resources of the institute, nevertheless, it accomplishes one of the other purposes of the dowry, and that is to provide a fund which insures a decent and respectable temporary subsistence for the sister, who, for any reason, leaves the institute and returns to the world.[10]

If the constitutions require a dowry, that dowry becomes subject to the regulations of the common law concerning its acquisition, investment, administration and restitution. The canons regulating these things speak of dowry in general, that is, without limiting it with respect to the type of religious institute.[11] Therefore, the superioresses of religious congregations, whether these be of pontifical or diocesan approval, as well as those of monasteries of nuns are bound by the prescriptions of the Code pertaining to the acquisition, investment, administration and restitution of the dotal funds.[12]

By virtue of canon 547, § 3, the constitutions of religious congregations are also free to specify regulations pertaining to the quality and quantity of the dowry, the time and manner of payment, and the special qualifications of candidates such as academic degrees or teachers' certificates which may be acceptable as a substitute for the dowry.[13]

That the law of dowry is compulsory in all monasteries of nuns and not in all congregations of sisters is explained in the divergence of the religious life led by these two classes of women religious.

---

[9] Cf. Vermeersch-Creusen, *loc. cit.;* Wernz-Vidal, *loc. cit.;* Larraona, "Commentarium Codicis,"—*CpRM,* XX (1939), 150-151; Bastien, *loc. cit.*

[10] Cf. Wernz-Vidal, *loc. cit.;* Bastien, *loc. cit.*

[11] Cf. canons 548-551.

[12] Cf. Larraona, *ibid.,* 148.

[13] Vermeersch-Creusen, *loc. cit.;* Toso, *loc. cit.;* Wernz-Vidal, *loc. cit.;* Oesterle, *Praelectiones Iuris Canonici,* I, 301; Vermeersch, "De Conscribendis Constitutionibus Congregationis Votorum Simplicium vel de iisdem ad Codicem Aptandis,"—*Periodica,* XVI (1927), 155*-156*; Creusen, *Religious Men and Women in the Code,* English translation by Garesche (3. English ed. by Ellis, Milwaukee: Bruce, 1940), p. 143, n. 185; Larraona, *ibid.,* 149-150; Bastien, *op. cit.,* p. 64, n. 99, and p. 65, n. 100; Beste, *Introductio in Codicem* (Collegeville: St. John's Abbey Press, 1938), p. 367.

The former observe the papal cloister and lead a contemplative life, which facts necessarily limit their participation in labors from which they can derive a means of support. For this reason they are forced to rely to a large extent on the income from their dowries to provide the necessities of life.[14] On the other hand, the members of societies with simple vows are not bound by the strict cloister and usually devote themselves to pious or charitable works from which they realize a financial income sufficient to meet, at least in a large measure, the expenses incurred by the community for their material sustenance. Therefore the dowry, as a source of income, is not so important to these religious as it is to those with solemn vows.[15]

Another reason for the compulsory law of dowry for monasteries of nuns is based on the juridical effect of the solemn vow of poverty taken by the nuns. By this vow they renounce irrevocably not only all goods which they possess,[16] but also every right to acquire further property in the future.[17] If one of these nuns leaves the monastery and returns to the world she cannot recover the property she once possessed, and therefore must rely on her dowry which will be refunded to her.[18] The same urgency is not always present when a sister departs from a religious congregation, for by her simple vow of poverty she does not renounce the ownership of her goods nor the capacity to acquire other goods.[19] Therefore, in the event of her departure she could rely on these goods for support.[20]

---

[14] Cf. Schaefer, *De Religiosis,* p. 502, n. 228; Wernz-Vidal, *op. cit.,* p. 222, footnote 16; Beste, *loc. cit.*

[15] Cf. Schaefer, *loc. cit.;* Wernz-Vidal, *loc. cit.;* Creusen-Garesche-Ellis, *op. cit.,* p. 143, n. 184.

[16] Canon 581, § 1.

[17] Canon 582.

[18] Canon 551, § 1.

[19] Canon 580, § 1.

[20] Cf. Eichmann, "Die Dos der Klosterfrau,"—*Theologie und Glaube,* XXVI (1934), 161.

ARTICLE III.   PAYMENT OF THE DOWRY

A. *In Monasteries of Nuns with Solemn Vows*

Canon 547, § 2: Haec dos ante susceptionem habitus monasterio tradatur aut saltem eius traditio tuta reddatur forma iure civili valida.

Immediately after imposing the obligation of a dowry in all monasteries of women with solemn vows,[21] the Code regulates the time and manner in which the payment must be made. The dowry shall be given to the monastery before the reception of the habit, or at least its payment must be guaranteed in a legal form recognized by the civil law.[22] These regulations have a direct application only to monasteries of solemn vows. This is evident from the opening words of canon 547, § 2, "this dowry" (*haec dos*), which necessarily refer to the preceding paragraph where the Code speaks of dowry in "monasteries of nuns" without any reference to congregations of women with simple vows. The latter are not mentioned until the third paragraph of the canon. Furthermore, paragraph 2 mentions specifically the payment of the dowry to the *monastery* and says nothing about *congregations*.[23] Therefore, it is evident that the regulations contained in canon 547, § 2, concerning the time and manner of the payment of the dowry are restricted to monasteries of women with solemn vows.[24] Nevertheless, the Sacred Congregation of Religious usually requires similar regulations to be inserted in the constitutions of congregations of sisters with simple vows.[25]

---

[21] Canon 547, § 1.

[22] Canon 547, § 2.

[23] Cf. canon 488, n. 2.

[24] Cf. Coronata, *Institutiones,* I, p. 725, n. 577; Vermeersch-Creusen, *Epitome,* I, p. 498, n, 699; Chelodi, *Ius de Persoris iuxta Codicem Iuris Canonici* (2. ed., Tridenti: Libr. Editr. Tridentum, 1927), p. 442, n. 267; Jardi, *El Derecho de las Religiosas según las Prescripciones Vigentes del Codigo Canónico y Civil* (2. ed., Vich: Serafica, 1927), p. 167, n. 450.

[25] Cf. *infra,* p. 58.

1) Actual Payment of the Dowry

Canon 547, § 2, provides for two acceptable methods in the payment of the dowry. The first is the actual delivery or handing over to the monastery of the required amount. The second consists in giving assurance of the actual payment in a form that is recognized and enforceable in civil law. The payment or the guarantee thereof must be made before the reception of the habit.

The wording of the canon implies, and reason dictates, that the first method is preferable. It is recognized, however, that circumstances will sometimes render the actual delivery of the dowry difficult or impossible at the time the candidate is prepared to be clothed with the habit, and therefore the Code allows an alternative by permitting an arrangement whereby the actual payment is deferred but nevertheless securely guaranteed.

The law requires that the payment, or the guarantee, be made to the monastery before the reception of the habit, or in other words, at the beginning of the novitiate. Canon 553 states that the novitiate begins with the reception of the habit, or in such other manner as is prescribed by the constitutions. In monasteries of nuns the novitiate always begins with the reception of the habit,[26] and therefore the dowry must be paid, or guaranteed, before the candidate is admitted to the novitiate.

Formerly the dowry was constituted at the beginning of the novitiate, but was not given to the monastery until after the novice had made profession. In the meantime it remained on deposit with a reliable person or with a bank.[27]

The decree *"Perpensis,"* which introduced into monasteries of nuns the three year term of simple vows before solemn profession, ordered that the dowry be paid to the monastery *before* simple profession, or, in other words, at the *end* of the novitiate, instead of *after* solemn profession as had been previously required.[28]

---

[26] Cf. Larraona, "Commentarium Codicis,"—*CpRM,* XX (1939), 146; Wernz-Vidal, *De Religiosis,* p. 233, n. 277.

[27] Cf. I Provincial Council of Milan (1565), *supra,* p. 18; S. C. Ep. et Reg., *Camerinen,* 2 dec. 1575, *supra,* p. 27; Clement XIII, const. *"Ci è stato,"* 13 febr. 1759, *supra,* p. 26.

[28] S. C. Ep. et Reg., 3 maii 1902—*Fontes,* n. 2039; *supra,* p. 28.

Canon 547, § 2, therefore, introduces another change when it requires the payment of the dowry to the monastery at the *beginning* of the novitiate. It will be noted that, in the process of the changes in the law relative to the delivery of the dowry to the monastery, the time for the constitution of the dowry has remained unchanged. From the first canonical legislation on the subject the law has remained constant in requiring the dowry to be constituted at the beginning of the novitiate.[29] In 1759 Clement XIII called attention to, and reaffirmed, the law in his constitution *"Ci è stato,"* when he took steps to abolish abuses whereby some monasteries followed the practice of admitting candidates to the novitiate before the latter had deposited their dowries as required by law.[30]

The necessity of paying the dowry before the beginning of the novitiate does not imply that the candidate must present it when she first takes up her life in the community. Canon 539 requires all women in religious organizations with perpetual vows to pass at least six months as postulants before they can be admitted to the novitiate. Therefore, the common law is complied with if the postulant supplies her dowry at any time before the expiration of that six months' period, or whatever other term may constitute the postulate in a particular monastery.[31] She may give it in one payment, or in installments provided the entire amount is paid before the reception of the habit, which act constitutes the canonical beginning of the novitiate.[32] In the event that the candidate fails for any reason to be professed the monastery has no right to the dowry whatsoever, and must return it to her.[33]

2) Promise of Payment

The second acceptable method for the payment of the dowry allows the candidate, in lieu of actual delivery of the money before the beginning of the novitiate, to furnish a legally enforceable

---

[29] Cf. *supra,* pp. 18, 26, 28.
[30] Bizzarri, *Coll. S. C. Ep. et Reg.,* pp. 34-35; cf. *supra,* p. 25.
[31] Cf. Blat, *Commentarium,* II, p. 311, n. 325.
[32] Canon 553.
[33] Cf. canon 570, § 2.

guarantee for the future payment. This arrangement is permitted as a convenience to the candidate or to those who assume the responsibility for the payment of her dowry. In allowing this procedure the Code is careful to take precautions to safeguard the interests of the monastery, and does so by demanding that the guarantee be drawn up in conformity with the civil law so that if necessary the execution may be enforced by a civil action.[34] The civil law formalities add nothing to the moral obligation of the fulfillment of the promise but merely constitute a guarantee for the protection of the rights of the monastery. A simple promise based on the good will of the promisor is not sufficient.[35] It must be drawn up in such a manner that it cannot be revoked; further, that, given the first profession of the novice, the payment becomes not only morally but civilly obligatory, irrespective of any contingencies, interpretations or objections.[36]

The Code gives only the general principle that the promise must be made in a form recognized in civil law. The precise form of the document is not determined and may vary by reason of the existing laws of the country in which it is drawn up. Most postulants are under 21 years of age and therefore come under the heading of minors. A practical point to keep in mind is that a personal promise or note of a minor is not enforceable in civil law. In those countries which do not recognize religious institutes as juridic personalities the promise would not be civilly enforceable if made to the institute as such. In these cases Vermeersch-Creusen[37] and other authors[38] say that the prescription of canon 547, § 2, is substantially complied with if in the legal

---

[34] Cf. canon 547, § 2; cf. also Toso, *Commentaria,* lib. II, pars II, p. 108, n. 3; Battandier, *Guide canonique* (1923), p. 143, n. 173; Larraona, "Commentarium Codicis,"—*CpRM,* XX (1939), 148.

[35] Schaefer, *De Religiosis,* p. 502, n. 228.

[36] Cf. Larraona, *ibid.,* 147-148; Toso, *loc. cit.;* Cocchi, *Commentarium in Codicem Iuris Canonici ad Usum Scholarum,* vol. IV (3. ed., Taurinorum Augustae: Marietti, 1932), p. 142, n. 67.

[37] *Loc. cit.*

[38] Coronata, *Institutiones,* I, p. 725, n. 577; Bastien, *Directoire canonique* (1923), p. 66, n. 101; Gerster, *Ius Religiosorum in Compendium Redactum* (Taurini: Marietti, 1935), 86; Toso, *loc. cit.*

promise the dowry is made payable to the superioress or to the persons who are recognized by the civil law as the possessors of the monastery. This difficulty is not important in the United States, because the law of this country permits the incorporation of religious institutes into legal entities. As such they may hold property and enforce their rights in the civil courts.

If the actual payment of the dowry is not made before the beginning of the novitiate, then at least the guarantee for the future payment must have been made at that time.[39] The law does not specify the exact time at which the promise of payment must be fulfilled. The extreme limit is implied in canon 549, which prescribes that the dowry be invested by the superioress after the first profession of the novice, and also in canon 551, § 1, which obliges the religious institute to return the dowry to a professed member who for any reason whatsoever leaves the community. In order to comply strictly with these laws it is evident that the monastery must have possession of the dowry at least shortly after the novice is professed. The jurisprudence before the Code was more explicit than the present law. Article 10 of the decree *"Perpensis"*[40] stated that in monasteries of nuns the prescribed dowry must be delivered to the monastery before simple profession. And article 93 of the *Normae* of 1901 contained a similar regulation for congregations of simple vows.

Although authors say that the money should be paid to the monastery before the first profession of the novice,[41] this is not expressly commanded in the present law. Nevertheless it would seem to be the most prudent and the preferable procedure from the practical point of view. If the term of the promise is not already provided for in the particular constitutions, it should be accurately defined in the document itself.

B. *In Religious Congregations of Sisters with Simple Vows*

As shown above,[42] the Code does not impose the necessity of a

---

[39] Cf. canon 547, § 2.
[40] S. C. Ep. et Reg., 3 maii 1902—*Fontes*, n. 2039.
[41] Ferreres, *Institutiones Canonicae* (2. ed., Barcinone, 1920), I, n. 857, II; Wernz-Vidal, *De Religiosis*, p. 224, n. 269; Coronata, *loc. cit.*
[42] *Supra*, p. 50.

dowry in congregations of sisters with simple vows, but rather commits its determination to the particular constitutions, both of pontifical and of diocesan institutes. Canon 547, § 3, gives them the liberty, not only to define in their constitutions whether or not a dowry shall be obligatory from the candidates seeking admission, but also to determine the manner and time of payment.[43] In practice, however, just as the Sacred Congregation of Religious in approving constitutions usually demands that at least a small dowry be made obligatory,[44] so also in regard to the manner and time of payment the same Congregation is accustomed to insert in the constitutions regulations similar to those required by the Code for monasteries of nuns with solemn vows.[45] Although canon 547, § 2, applies directly only to monasteries,[46] the prescriptions of that paragraph concerning the manner and time of payment of the dowry constitute a directive norm for congregations.[47] The constitutions of many religious institutes of sisters with simple vows, following article 93 of the *Normae* of 1901, order that the dowry be guaranteed before the reception of the habit and paid before profession.[48]

The same reasons as those given for monasteries[49] urge the congregations to demand that the dowry be paid or at least guaranteed before the reception of the habit. This will obviate the unpleasant and embarrassing situation which would arise if, at the end of the novitiate, the profession of a novice had to

---

[43] Toso, *Commentaria*, lib. II, pars II, p. 108, n. 4; Blat, *Commentarium*, II, p. 312, n. 325; Vermeersch-Creusen, *Epitome*, I, p. 498, n. 699; Chelodi, *Ius de Personis*, p. 442, footnote 2; Cappello, *Summa Iuris Canonici in Usum Scholarum Concinnata*, Vol. II (3. ed., Romae: Universitas Gregoriana, 1939), p. 204, n. 604; DeMeester, *Juris Canonici et Juris Canonico-Civilis Compendium*, Vol. II (nova ed., Brugis, 1923), p. 436, art. 995 (hereafter this work will be cited as *Compendium*).

[44] Cf. *supra*, p. 50.

[45] Vermeersch-Creusen, *loc. cit.*; Larraona, "Commentarium Codicis,"— *CpRM*, XX (1939), p. 150, IV; and footnote 685. Cf. also canon 547, § 2, [46] Cf. *supra*, p. 53.

[47] Coronata, *Institutiones*, I, p. 725, n. 577; Wernz-Vidal, *De Religiosis*, p. 224, n. 269; Chelodi, *Ius De Personis*, p. 442, footnote 2.

[48] Chelodi, *loc. cit.*

[49] Cf. *supra*, p. 57.

be postponed because she was unable to pay the necessary dowry.

If the constitutions permit a guarantee at the beginning of the novitiate for the future payment, they may or may not require the agreement to be drawn up in a manner which is valid in the civil law. In any case actual payment should be required by the time of profession, in order that the investment of the capital may be made as prescribed by canon 549.

Since no legislation is contained in the common law on the manner and time of the payment of the dowry in congregations of sisters with simple vows, expediency demands and common sense dictates that the constitutions be definite and precise in the matter.

CHAPTER VI

CONSTITUTION OF THE DOWRY

ARTICLE I. QUALITY

The close unanimity among the authors in defining the necessity of a dowry in religious institutes of women is lacking when these same authors discuss the quality of the dowry, or in other words, its material constituents. Many divergent opinions exist in regard to the nature of that which is acceptable for constituting the dowry. The Code is silent on the matter, as were also the *Normae* of 1901. The principal dispute centers around the question of whether or not the dowry must consist in money (*pecunia numerata*), as was the generally accepted rule before the promulgation of the Code. The Sacred Congregation of Bishops and Regulars had stated on different occasions that the dowry must be paid in money; and the authors before the Code accepted this as establishing a general norm.[1]

The question now arises whether or not the Code, by its failure to specify the quality of the dowry, has introduced any change in the law. Some authors without expressly discussing the point imply by their definitions of dowry that the former law is still in force. Gerster[2] and Cocchi[3] in defining dowry call it a "sum of money" (*pecuniae summa*) which the postulant gives to the monastery for her support. Ferreres says that it must be paid in money unless a dispensation is obtained.[4] Blat adheres to the former law but is willing to admit some modifications. He states that the investment of the dowry in securities as required by canon 549 cannot be made except with money, and therefore holds that the former law is still obligatory. If productive immovable goods,

---

[1] Cf. *supra*, p. 32.
[2] *Ius Religiosorum*, p. 85.
[3] *Commentarium*, IV, p. 142, n. 67.
[4] *Institutiones Canonicae*, I, p. 393, n. 857, IV.

such as land or a house, are offered, he says they may be accepted as payment for the dowry, provided they are sold before the profession of the novice at a price which amounts to at least as much as the dowry which is required by custom or the constitutions of the institute. Blat also admits that securities equivalent in value to the amount of the dowry are permitted if such investments have the approval of the superioress and her council, and the consent of the local ordinary and, if the house is subject to regulars, of the regular superior, in order that the prescriptions of canon 549 may be fulfilled.[5]

Most authors do not restrict the payment to money, properly so called, but in varying degrees admit other classes of securities which to all practical purposes may be considered as the equivalent of money. For example, Cappello[6] and Battandier[7] say that ordinarily the dowry is to be paid in money, to which title-deeds, stocks and bonds are considered as equivalent. Vromant,[8] following Fanfani,[9] admits besides money "temporal goods" for constituting the dowry, as also do Chelodi[10] and Beste.[11] Vermeersch-Creusen[12] and DeMeester[13] define it as "capital or productive goods . . . ," and Pruemmer[14] as a "sum of money or other productive goods. . . ." The term "productive goods" as used by these authors undoubtedly includes such securities as first mortgages, notes, stocks, bonds, etc. Augustine says that the dowry must be paid in money or its equivalent, and adds that "any secure source of income, either money or title-deeds, government or state bonds, bank deposits or shares in sound stock companies are admissible."[15]

---

[5] *Commentarium*, II, p. 316, n. 337.
[6] *Summa*, II, p. 203, n. 604.
[7] *Guide canonique* (1923), p. 142, n. 173.
[8] *De Bonis Ecclesiae Temporalibus*, p. 267, n. 251.
[9] *De Iure Religiosorum ad Normam Codicis Iuris Canonici* (2. ed., Taurini-Romae: Marietti, 1925), p. 188, n. 167.
[10] *Ius de Personis*, p. 442, n. 267.
[11] *Introductio in Codicem*, p. 367.
[12] *Epitome*, I, p. 497, n. 698.
[13] *Compendium*, II, 436.
[14] *Manuale Iuris Canonici*, p. 276, Q. 208, 1.
[15] *A Commentary on the New Code of Canon Law*, III, 225.

Departing further from the former law, Creusen[16] and Cance[17] accept "movable or immovable capital." Coronata in his definition of dowry speaks of it as a "sum of money or goods . . ." and says that besides money properly so called, often consumable things are also prescribed for the dowry.[18] As will be shown below, even though such articles are prescribed by custom or by the constitutions of the institute, they are not to be reckoned as dowry properly so called.[19]

Goyeneche discusses the case of a postulant who has neither the money nor any securities with which to pay her dowry, but who has real estate which cannot be sold here and now. He says that nowhere in the Code is it stated that a postulant cannot bring as a dowry movable or immovable goods as equivalent for money. By reason of the definitions of dowry as given by modern authors, which definitions depart from the one that was implied by the strict regulation of the old law which demanded that the dowry be constituted in money, and also by reason of the fact that the old law is not shown to be contained either explicitly or implicitly in the Code, Goyeneche permits the postulant to discharge her obligation of paying the dowry by transferring the property to the monastery. The monastery is then obliged to sell it and invest the price in securities according to the law of canon 549.[20] Schaefer follows the same opinion.[21] Other authors even permit the institute to retain the real estate as an invested dowry, provided it constituted a safe, lawful and productive investment.[22] Some admit, however, that real estate is less desirable because of the more complex problems of administering it. Furthermore, it is less suitable in accomplishing the purpose of the dowry, and if

---

[16] *Religieux et Religieuses d'apres le droit ecclesiastique* (3. ed., Bruxelles: Dewitt, 1924), p. 137, n. 150.

[17] *Le Code de droit canonique,* II (Paris: Gabalda et Fils, 1928), 66.

[18] *Institutiones,* I, p. 724, n. 577.

[19] Cf. *infra,* p. 66.

[20] "Consultationes,"—*CpRM,* XI (1930), 37-38.

[21] *De Religiosis,* p. 501, n. 228.

[22] Wernz-Vidal, *De Religiosis,* p. 221, n. 267; Cappello, *Summa,* II, pp. 203-204, n. 604; Jombart, "Une dot qui consisterait en une maison,"—*Revue des communautés religieuses,* I (1925), 158; Bastien, *Directoire canonique* (1923), p. 66, n. 101.

real estate is accepted, then the laws regulating the dowry become more difficult of fulfillment.[23]

The absence of a general law on the point and the variation of opinion among the modern authors make it impossible to set forth a hard and fast rule stating precisely those things which are acceptable for constituting the dowry and excluding those which are not acceptable. Apparently it was the mind of the legislator to leave a certain amount of latitude to the judgment of those whose duty it is to accept and administer the dowries, due account being taken by them of special circumstances.

Ordinarily, the payment will be made in money, and unquestionably this manner of payment is to be preferred, for the prescriptions of the law governing the investment, administration and restitution of the dowry are thereby made easier to observe, and the rights of the members who leave the institute either before or after profession can thereby be more readily safeguarded. The particular constitutions usually imply that the dowry be paid in money, for they speak of the dowry in terms of money and not in terms of securities or immovable goods.[24] However, there seems to be no reason to reject as payment for the dowry such securities as those mentioned by Augustine,[25] that is, title deeds, government or state bonds, bank deposits and shares in sound stock companies. For these securities, if sound, are accepted in the financial world as practically the equivalent of money. Furthermore, since the dowry if paid in actual money must be invested after profession in securities similar to the above, these same types of securities should be acceptable for the payment itself, provided of course they measure up to the qualifications enumerated in canon 549 for the investment of dowries. They must be safe, lawful and productive, and made by the superioress after consulting her council and after obtaining the consent of the local ordinary and, if the monastery is subject to regulars, of the regular superior.[26]

---

[23] Cf. Wernz-Vidal, *loc. cit.*; Jombart, *loc. cit.*,
[24] Cf. Larraona, "Commentarium Codicis,"—*CpRM,* XX (1939), 14-15, IV.
[25] Cf. *supra,* p. 61.
[26] Cf. canons 549 and 533, § 1, nn. 1-2.

As stated above, congregations with simple vows have by reason of canon 547, § 3, the liberty to specify in their constitutions the nature or quality of the dowry, subject of course to the approval of the Sacred Congregation of Religious if the institute be one that has pontifical approval or to the local ordinary if the institute be one which has but diocesan approval.[27] In the absence of any specific provisions in the constitutions congregations of sisters are bound by the same norms as monasteries of nuns in regard to the quality of the dowry. Constitutions sometimes provide that a girl with a teacher's certificate or some similar evidence of special qualifications may be admitted without the payment of a dowry. Some authors speak of such a certificate as the equivalent of a dowry,[28] but it is difficult to see how, apart from special provisions in the constitutions, it can be accepted for a dowry properly so called.[29] It is true that the reception of a candidate thus qualified is a distinct advantage to the community and may represent a financial saving often in excess of the actual amount of the dowry, but when the certificate is considered in the light of the three principal purposes of the dowry it is found wanting. In the first place, the dowry is intended to supply an income upon which the community may depend for at least a part of the cost of supporting the one who brought it. Now a teacher's certificate is, of itself, unproductive, and if anything should hinder the sister from teaching the certificate would be useless. Secondly, the law states that on the death of the religious, the capital of the dowry accrues to the institute.[30] No such benefit is derived by an institute, however, on the death of a religious who had been admitted with the certificate as a substitute for the dowry. Finally, the dowry consists in a fund which guarantees a respectable and decent temporary living for a religious who, for any reason whatsoever, leaves the institute. It is true that the certificate would

---

[27] Cf. *supra*, p. 51.

[28] Cf. Cappello, *Summa*, p. 203, n. 604; Coronata, *Institutiones*, I, p. 724, n. 577.

[29] Cf. Fanfani, *De Iure Religiosorum*, p. 189, n. 168, Dubium I; Vromant, *De Bonis Ecclesiae Temporalibus*, p. 267, n. 251; Blat, *Commentarium*, II, p. 313, n. 328.

[30] Canon 548.

enable the secularized religious to qualify for a teaching position, but it would not of itself take care of her support immediately after her departure when she would, in all probability, need it most.[31]

Furthermore, anything to qualify as dowry should be such that the regulations of canons 549-551 can be observed. The nature of a teacher's certificate excludes any possibility of its being invested as canon 549 prescribes for the dowry. And the regulations for the administration of dowries as contained in canon 550, as well as the provisions in canon 551 for the restoration of the dowry to a departing religious, would have little meaning or application. Because of the advantages to the religious community, however, some constitutions provide for the acceptance of a candidate endowed with a teacher's certificate or similar qualification in lieu of a dowry. In other cases, it would often happen that such qualifications of a candidate would be ample cause for seeking a dispensation from the dowry.[32] Vromant[33] and Creusen[34] wisely advise against too frequent use of substituting for the dowry a teacher's certificate or some similar qualification because of the consequent inconveniences to both the community and the religious.

Not to be confused with dowry are unconditional gifts made to the convent by a candidate while she has the juridical right to dispose of her property. A gift or donation by its very nature becomes permanent and irrevocable when it is accepted by the party to whom it is offered. Therefore, gifts made to and accepted by the convent cannot be recovered in the manner of the capital of the dowry if the candidate leaves the convent. The special law of canon 551, § 1, which requires the restitution of the dowry to a departing religious, does not extend to gifts or donations.[35]

---

[31] Cf. Creusen-Garesché-Ellis, *Religious Men and Women in the Code,* p. 143, n. 185; Vromant, *loc. cit.;* Geser, *The Canon Law Governing Communities of Sisters* (St. Louis: Herder, 1938), p. 210, Q. 657.

[32] Cf. Vromant, *loc. cit.;* Fanfani, *op. cit.,* p. 189, n. 168, Dubium I; Schaefer, *De Religiosis,* p. 503, n. 228.

[33] *Loc. cit.*

[34] *Loc. cit.*

[35] Cf. Battandier, *op. cit.,* p. 147, n. 178; Schaefer, *loc. cit.;* Fanfani, *op. cit.,* p. 192, n. 171, Dubium III; Bastien, *Directoire canonique* (1923), p. 67, n. 101.

Canon 570, § 1, states that no compensation may be claimed for the expenditures of keeping a postulant or novice, except what the constitutions perhaps demand for food and clothing, or what was agreed upon for these purposes by explicit contract at the beginning of the postulate or novitiate. Whatever is paid to the community in accordance with this canon should not be confused with dowry. It is entirely distinct from and in addition to the dowry. Its purpose is to defray the expenses of the postulate and novitiate, while the dowry consists in a capital sum, the income from which contributes to the support of the religious after profession.[36] Furthermore, canon 570, § 1, applies to religious institutes of men as well as of women,[37] while the dotal law applies only to the latter.

The second paragraph of canon 570 demands that whatever the candidate brought and has not actually consumed by use must be returned if she does not make profession but returns to the world. If the constitutions or custom of the institute require the candidate to bring linens, clothing and other similar equipment, a record of these articles should be kept so that they may be returned if the candidate fails to make profession.[38] It is incorrect to maintain with some authors, including Coronata[39] and Leitner,[40] that such articles and supplies can constitute a dowry. It is entirely lawful for the constitutions or a standing custom to prescribe the bringing of these articles which by their very nature are unproductive and consumed with use, but they should not be

---

[36] Cf. Larraona, "Commentarium Codicis,"—*CpRM*, XX (1939), 10. Cocchi uses the word "dowry" in a broad and improper sense when he says that many communities of sisters demand a dowry only for the support of the novice during the novitiate: "in multis religionibus sororum dos exigitur tantum pro sustentatione tempore novitiatus";—*Commentarium*, IV, p. 142, n. 67.

[37] Cf. canon 490.

[38] Wernz-Vidal, *De Religiosis*, p. 228, n. 272; Schaefer, *De Religiosis*, p. 501, n. 228.

[39] *Institutiones*, I, p. 724, n. 577.

[40] *Handbuch des katholischen Kirchenrechts*, Dritte Lieferung: *Das Ordensrecht* (2. ed., Regensburg: Kösel und Pustet, 1922), p. 391. (Hereafter this work will be cited as *Das Ordensrecht*.)

considered as dowry.[41] They fail to measure up to the nature and purpose of a dowry for reasons similar to those given above in the exclusion of teachers' certificates.[42]

ARTICLE II.   QUANTITY

Just as the Code fails to specify the quality of the dowry, so also it remains silent regarding the determination of the quantity to be paid by the candidates when they enter religion.   This silence of the Code is not surprising, for it must be remembered that the Code constitutes a body of permanent laws written for, and binding on, the Universal Church.   Consequently, it could not be expected to contain detailed regulations on matters subject to such variations as the quantity of the dowry.   And so the legislator makes allowance for the adjustment and regulation of the amount of the dowry by committing its determination to the constitutions or legitimate customs of individual religious institutes.

Thus canon 547, § 1, states that in monasteries of nuns the postulant must bring the dowry required by the constitutions or determined by legitimate custom.   And paragraph three of the same canon states that in regard to the dowry in congregations of simple vows the constitutions must be followed.   This flexibility of the general law of the Code permits allowance to be made for numerous circumstances in establishing the amount of dowry in a given institute.

The lack of a more definite general law does not mean that religious institutes have an uncontrolled freedom in determining the amount of the dowry.   Whatever amount is specified by the constitutions and whatever be the method or manner employed in the determination of this amount, the approval of the proper ecclesiastical authority is required before the rule which is thus invoked actually becomes binding.   The constitutions of all pontifical communities are approved by the Sacred Congregation of Religious, and those of all diocesan communities by the local

---

[41] Cf. Larraona, "Commentarium Codicis,"—*CpRM*, XX (1939), 11, footnote 600.

[42] Cf. *supra*, pp. 64-65.

ordinary. Thus it is seen that while the Code refrains from indicating the amount of the dowry to be established in religious institutes, the Church nevertheless exercises a very definite control over the matter by requiring approval of all constitutions by the proper ecclesiastical authority.

In drawing up the constitutions of a religious institute all the factors should be considered which will aid in determining the most suitable amount of dowry to be demanded from the candidates. For example, a given amount may be adequate in one region or at one time, but entirely unsatisfactory elsewhere or at another time, because of diverse economic and financial conditions. It is evident that a larger dowry should be prescribed for contemplative orders than for those in which the members lead an active life.[43] The latter usually engage in works such as conducting schools, hospitals, orphanages, etc., and from these enterprises earn an income which is often sufficient to defray the expenses incurred for their material support. In contemplative orders, on the contrary, the religious life is incompatible with such occupations, and therefore the members must rely to a greater extent on the income from the invested dowries. Even in the same type of religious institutes the extent of the need of a dowry may vary greatly, for instance, when an institute is richly endowed and thereby largely self-supporting apart from the income received from the dowries.

In congregations of sisters with simple vows the prescribed dowry is often so small that the annual income from it is almost negligible as compared to the cost of supporting a religious. For example, some congregations require a dowry of $100. In the event that this amount is invested to yield a 4% return, the $4.00 received annually would be far from adequate to meet the yearly cost of supplying the most meagre existence. Although the primary end of the dowry is to provide an income for the maintenance of the professed religious, in most cases the capital is not sufficient to yield a return which will cover the entire cost of support, but rather only a portion of it. The balance must be

---

[43] Schaefer, *De Religiosis,* p. 502, n. 228; Wernz-Vidal, *De Religiosis,* p. 222, footnote 16; Creusen-Garesché-Ellis, *Religious Men and Women in the Code,* p. 143, n. 184; Gerster, *Ius Religiosorum,* p. 86.

gathered from other sources such as the labors of the religious, donations, endowments, etc.

Articles 91 of the *Normae* of 1901 made a dowry obligatory in every institute, permitting, however, a lesser amount to be paid by the lay sisters than by the choir sisters. It provided further that the amount be equal for each member of the respective class. The Code, however, does not contain these requirements. Particular constitutions sometimes make definite provisions for a variation of the amount to be asked from candidates for the same religious congregation. For example, because of the present economic difficulties throughout the world, the General Chapter may be given permission to determine the dowry in the various houses of the institute.[44] It is evident that diverse economic conditions call for a variation in the amount of the dowry to be asked from candidates seeking admission into a religious institute which has houses in Europe, Asia and America. The General Chapter of the institute is best suited to consider the conditions in each region and adjust the dowry accordingly.

The determination of the dowry in the constitutions may be fixed and absolute (e.g., $100), or it may be variable and relative so that only the manner of determining it is given (e.g., by the General Chapter).[45] The freedom accorded to congregations of simple vows in canon 547, § 3, enables such institutes not only to determine whether or not a dowry shall be obligatory, but also to specify details pertaining to the manner in which the amount is determined. Constitutions sometimes contain such provisions as the following: That a larger dowry be required from the choir sisters than from the lay sisters; that it be procured if possible; that the amount be determined by the General Chapter; that for just causes it may be diminished by the major superioress; that it be constituted from a legitimate part of the inheritance of the

---

[44] Vermeersch-Creusen, *Epitome,* I, p. 497, n. 698; Vermeersch, "De Dotis Quantitate Definienda,"—*Periodica,* XII (1923), (162): ". . . Quare, ni fallimur, articulus de dote iam hoc modo in novis constitutionibus scribi permittetur: Dotis exigendae quantitas decreto capituli generalis, habita quoque varia regionum condicione, definitur."

[45] Vermeersch-Creusen, *loc. cit.;* Toso, *Commentaria,* lib. II, pars II, p. 108, n. 4.

candidate; that a teacher's certificate or similar qualification be accepted as a substitute.[46]

Unless it be forbidden by the constitutions, a candidate may, with the consent of the superioress, give a larger sum as a dowry than the amount specified. In this case the total amount becomes subject to the dotal law of the Code. In other words, the excess over and above the regular dowry is acquired, invested, administered, transferred or restored along with that part which corresponds to the amount required by the constitutions or custom.[47]

---

[46] Cf. Vermeersch-Creusen, *loc. cit.;* Schaefer, *op. cit.,* p. 502, n. 228; Wernz-Vidal, *op. cit.,* p. 223, n. 268; Bastien, *Directoire canonique* (1923), p. 64, n. 99; Oesterle, *Praelectiones Iuris Canonici,* I, 301; Vermeersch, "De Conscribendis Constitutionibus Congregationis Votorum Simplicium vel de iisdem ad Codicem Aptandis," II, 3, "De Dote,"—*Periodica* XVI (1927), 155*-156*.

[47] Schaefer, *op. cit.,* p. 501, footnote 291; Vermeersch-Creusen, *op. cit.,* I, p. 498, n. 698; Larraona, *ibid.,* p. 11; Coronata, *op. cit.,* I, pp. 724-725, n. 577.

CHAPTER VII

CONDONATION OF THE DOWRY

Canon 547, § 4: Dos praescripta condonari ex toto vel ex parte nequit sine indulto Sanctae Sedis, si agatur de religione iuris pontificii; sine venia Ordinarii loci, si de religione iuris dioecesani.

Canon 547, § 4, lends support to the laws designating the necessity of a dowry by providing that the prescribed dowry cannot be condoned, either in whole or in part, without an indult from the Holy See in pontifical institutes, or without permission from the local ordinary in diocesan institutes. The source from which the obligation of paying a dowry arises is immaterial. That is to say that the law forbidding condonation applies equally to all religious institutes in which a dowry is obligatory, whether the obligation arises from the common law or from the particular constitutions.[1] Therefore, the law forbidding condonation is always applicable to monasteries of nuns, because the Code itself[2] decrees the necessity of a dowry in all monasteries of nuns with solemn vows. The same cannot be said of congregations, whether pontifical or diocesan, because by common law they enjoy the liberty of determining in their constitutions whether or not a dowry shall be obligatory and whether or not any power of condonation be committed to the superioress or to some specified governing body within the institute, provided ecclesiastical authority has sanctioned this ruling.[3]

---

[1] Vermeersch-Creusen, *Epitome,* I, p. 498, n. 698; Coronata, *Institutiones,* I, p. 725, n. 577; Schaefer, *De Religiosis,* p. 503, footnote 297; Wernz-Vidal, *De Religiosis,* p. 223, n. 268; Toso, *Commentaria,* lib. II, pars II, p. 108, n. 5; Chelodi, *Ius de Personis,* p. 442, n. 267; Oesterle, *Praelectiones Iuris Canonici,* I, 301.

[2] Canon 547, § 1.

[3] Cf. canon 547, § 3; cf. also Schaefer, *op. cit.,* p. 502, n. 228; Wernz-Vidal, *loc. cit.;* Creusen, "Dispense de la dot," *Revue des Communautés*

Three possibilities may be considered:

1). The constitutions may contain no mention whatsoever of a dowry, or may even say expressly that none shall be required. With no dowry prescribed, naturally there can be no question of condonation, and the problem presents no difficulties. As treated in a previous chapter, the Sacred Congregation of Religious is reluctant to approve a set of constitutions unless at least a small dowry is called for.[4]

2). The constitutions may impose the obligation of a dowry absolutely and without making any special provision for its condonation in particular cases. Canon 547, § 4, has a direct application to such an institute, because the expression "prescribed dowry" of this law embraces congregations relative to which the prescription is contained in the particular constitutions as well as monasteries for which the dowry is prescribed by the common law. Unless the faculty to dispense from the dowry is contained expressly in the constitutions, no one except those mentioned in canon 547, § 4, can dispense from it.[5] Therefore, no superioress or governing body within the institute can dispense from the dowry, either in whole or in part. The power of dispensation is reserved to the proper ecclesiastical authority, depending on the type of institute, that is, whether pontifical or diocesan. If pontifical, the Sacred Congregation of Religious is competent; if diocesan, the local ordinary. Frequently the Sacred Congregation of Religious grants an adult to institutes for a definite number of cases.[6]

3). The constitutions may prescribe a dowry, but at the same time use the freedom allowed them by canon 547, § 3, and commit certain powers of condonation to the superioress or some governing body in the institute. In this case the prohibition, as contained

---

Religieuses, III (1927), 133; Vermeersch-Creusen, *op. cit.,* I, p. 497, n. 698; Creusen-Garesché-Ellis, *Religious Men and Women in the Code,* p. 143, n. 185; Larraona, "Commentarium Codicis,"—*CpRM,* XX (1939), 150.

[4] Cf. *supra,* p. 50.

[5] Cf. Larraona, *ibid.,* p. 152; Toso, *op. cit.,* lib. II, pars II, p. 108, n. 5.

[6] Bastien, *Directoire canonique* (1923), p. 64, n. 100; Battandier, *Guide canonique* (1923), p. 144, n. 175; Blat, *Commentarium,* II, p. 312, n. 325; Vermeersch-Creusen, *op. cit.,* I, p. 498, n. 698.

in canon 547, § 4, of condoning the dowry is necessarily limited to the extent of the dispensatory powers given by the approved constitutions to the superioress or others. It is obvious that if the constitutions give the power to the superioress she needs no further authority to act. The permission of the Holy See or of the local ordinary need not be obtained.[7]

A great diversity in the dispensing powers of religious superioresses is found in the various particular constitutions.[8] This is not surprising in view of the freedom given in canon 547, § 3, to both pontifical and diocesan congregations of simple vows in respect to the dowry. Because of peculiar circumstances in individual cases the provisions similar to those described in the latter of the three cases mentioned above are valuable and useful to the community, provided of course that the power is not abused. More or less frequent cases may occur when it redounds to the benefit of a community to receive a girl without a dowry. The usual example given is the case of a candidate endowed with some special qualification such as a teacher's certificate or nurse's degree. The advantages of her services to the community compensate for her reception without a dowry.[9]

The mere fact of a candidate's value to the community, however, is not sufficient of itself to set aside the law which establishes the necessity of a dowry, whether this law be the law of the Code or a ruling incorporated in the constitutions. Recourse must be had to the authority endowed with the power of dispensing. If the constitutions give that power to the superioress, she may act precisely within the limits and according to the faculties which she possesses.[10]

---

[7] Creusen-Garesché-Ellis, *op. cit.,* pp. 143-144, n. 185; Oesterle, *Praelectiones Iuris Canonici,* I, 301; Geser, *The Canon Law Governing Communities of Sisters,* p. 211, q. 660.

[8] Cf. Larraona, *ibid.,* p. 150, footnote 686; Bastien, *op. cit.,* p. 64, n. 99; Vermeersch, "De Conscribendis Constitutionibus Congregationis Votorum Simplicium vel de iisdem ad Codicem Aptandis,"—*Periodica,* XVI (1927), 156*.

[9] Wernz-Vidal, *De Religiosis,* p. 223, n. 268; Vermeersch, *loc. cit.;* Leitner, *Das Ordensrecht,* p. 390.

[10] For example, the constitutions may give her unrestricted power, or they may state the restricted causes which entitle her to grant the dispensation either in whole or in part.

The local ordinary has, by common law, the power to condone the dowry prescribed by the constitutions of diocesan institutes.[11] Furthermore, he has, by virtue of the quinquennial faculties from the Holy See, the power "to dispense from the want of dowry, in whole or in part, in the case of nuns or sisters [of pontifical institutes], provided that the financial condition of the institute does not suffer thereby, and that the applicants have such qualifications that they give certain promise of being of great service to the institute."[12]

This faculty gives the local ordinary power to dispense from the dowry in any pontifical institute, whether the religious profess solemn or simple vows. He may exercise it only under two conditions: first, that the financial condition of the institute does not suffer as a result of the dispensation; and secondly, that the applicant has such qualifications that her admission will be highly useful to the institute.[13] From the nature of these conditions it is evident that each case must be considered individually and decided on its own merits.

The Apostolic Delegate possesses broader power of dispensing from the dowry than the local ordinary. By virtue of his faculties he may "dispense, for a just cause at the request of the community, as regards the want of dowry required for sisters or nuns in religion."[14] A just cause may arise from such sources as the special merits of the postulant, her usefulness to the institute, or the fact that the institute has sufficient financial resources.[15] If there is present a just cause similar to those enumerated the Apostolic Delegate may, at the request of the community, grant

---

[11] Canon 547, § 4.

[12] IV, Faculties from the Sacred Congregation of Religious, n. 5— Bouscaren, *The Canon Law Digest,* II, 12.

[13] Cf. Creusen, "Dispense de la dot,"—*Revue des Commun. Relig.,* III (1927), 133; Papi, *Religious in Church Law* (New York, Kenedy, 1924), 99.

[14] Chapter V, Faculties Relating to Religious, n. 47—Bouscaren, *The Canon Law Digest,* I, 184.

[15] "Facultatum quae, post Codicem, Legatis Apostolicis Concedi Consueverunt breve Commentarium,"—*Periodica,* XII (1923), (144).

a dispensation from the dowry, even a general dispensation if the same conditions are fulfilled in each case.[16]

When a dispensation has been granted to a postulant who was unable to pay the prescribed dowry, she is freed once and for all from the obligation of paying it, even though later on, either before or after profession, she comes into the possession of wealth.[17] The reason is that a dispensation from the dowry does not have a recurrent application and therefore in accordance with the norm of canon 86, after the execution of the rescript, it liberates one from the obligation of the law which does not revive even though the causes for which it was granted cease.[18] Unless the contrary is expressly stated in the constitutions or agreed to by mutual consent, the dispensation is absolute and is independent of the future change in the financial condition of the candidate. Creusen advises that dispensations be granted conditionally, that is, with the obligation of paying the dowry later if the candidate is able to do so.[19]

A dispensation granted by a superioress to whom dispensatory power has not been conceded is invalid.[20] This, however, does not make the novitiate invalid, for although the dotal law is contained in the Code under the article entitled: "The Requisites for One to be Admitted to the Novitiate," the dowry is not listed among the things required for the validity of the novitiate.[21]

The Code does not distinguish which local ordinary is intended in canon 547, § 4. Is it the ordinary of the place where the major or provincial superioress has her headquarters, or is it the ordinary of the place in which the novitiate is situated? Ver-

---

[16] *Loc. cit.*

[17] Larraona, "De Dote Religiosarum in Codice Iuris Canonici,"—*CpRM,* XIX (1938), 99; Schaefer, *De Religiosis,* p. 503, n. 228; Geser, *The Canon Law Governing Communities of Sisters,* p. 211, q. 661.

[18] Cf. Larraona, "Consultationes,"—*CpRM,* IX (1928), 326; Schaefer, *loc. cit.*

[19] "Dispense de la dot,"—*Revue des communautés religieuses,* III (1927), 133; Creusen-Garesché-Ellis, *Religious Men and Women in the Code,* p. 144, n. 185.

[20] Cf. canon 80.

[21] Cf. canons 542, 555, 556.

meersch[22] and Blat[23] restrict it to the ordinary of the place of
the novitiate, and Toso simply points to the ordinary of the place
where the religious house is found.[24]   Larraona says that in the
absence of any specific distinction on this matter in the Code
it may be concluded that both the one and the other of the two
local ordinaries are competent to grant the dispensation from the
dowry.[25]   Correspondingly the dispensation may be granted either
by the ordinary in whose diocese the house of the novitiate is
situated or by the ordinary in whose diocese the superioress who
admits the postulant to the novitiate has her residence.   Larraona's expressed view which preferably concedes the competence
here in question to the latter of these two ordinaries appears to
be the more logical one, for the dowries are to be administered, not
at the novitiate, but at the habitual residence of the major or provincial superioress.[26]   Furthermore, it is the ordinary of the place
where the major or provincial superioress has her habitual residence
who has the duty of vigilance over the dotal funds.[27]

Arguments can be given in support of an exceptional case
wherein the law of canon 547, § 4, is not binding.   Before the
Code authors generally held that if a monastery of nuns had
real need of a candidate, for example, of a lay religious to perform
domestic duties, she could be received without a dowry, even
though no special faculty to that effect was possessed by the
superioress either from the common law or from the constitutions.[28]
Canon 547, § 4, contains a restatement of the old law prohibiting

---

[22] "De Conscribendis Constitutionibus Congregationis Votorum Simplicium
vel de iisdem ad Codicem Aptandis,"—*Periodica,* XVI (1927), 156*.
[23] *Commentarium,* II, p. 312, n. 325.
[24] *Commentaria,* lib. II, pars II, p. 108, n. 5.
[25] "Commentarium Codicis,"—*CpRM,* XX (1939), 155.
[26] Cf. canon 550, § 1.
[27] Cf. canon 550, § 2.
[28] Cf. S. C. Ep. et Reg., 20 mart. 1594—Ferraris, "Moniales," II, n. 18;
Pellizzarius, *De Monialibus,* c. III, sect. II, n. 46; Petra, *Commentaria,*
III, const. XII, Innocentii IV (*Solet annuere*), sect. I, n. 54; Vermeersch,
De Religiosis Institutis et Personis, I, pars IV, sect. I, c. II, n. 181;
Goyeneche, "Consultationes,"—*CpRM,* XI (1930), 37; Lucidi, *De Visitatione,* II, c. V, § 5, n. 186. Lucidi adds that in practice an indult was
usually obtained.

the condonation of the dowry in monasteries of nuns. Therefore it must be interpreted, as canon 6, in nn. 2 and 3, directs, in accordance with the old law; and hence the interpretation accepted by approved authors is to be followed in the interpretation of this law of the Code. Applying this rule of interpretation[29] Larraona[30] asserts that a monastery which has special need of a religious for a determined office may receive her without a dowry.[31] In the application of this interpretation caution should be the watchword in order to avoid abuses and to prevent the violation of the ordinance of canon 547, § 4. It was an extraordinary procedure in the old law, and must remain the same under the present law. Certainly, resort to this procedure would not be permitted if the candidate could pay the dowry, or if another qualified candidate who could pay was available.

A number of practical cases may arise in which the postulant is unable to pay the dowry but nevertheless may be received without a dispensation because the amount of the dowry is supplied from some other source. For example, when a religious, in arranging for the administration of her property during the term of her simple profession,[32] provides that the income be used to constitute a dowry for another candidate; or when a benefactor of the monastery leaves a sum of money to constitute a dowry; or when a candidate, upon entering, contributes an amount sufficient to constitute another dowry with the express condition that it be used for paying the dowry of a poor girl. In the latter case the condition must be specified before, or at least at, the time the money is paid to the monastery. For if the excess is given as an unconditional gift it becomes incorporated into the goods of

---

[29] This should not be confused with those cases in which the community has the right by reason of an immemorial custom to admit lay nuns without a dowry.

[30] "Commentarium Codicis,"—*CpRM,* XX (1939), 152.

[31] Some authors mention such need on the part of the monastery as a cause for seeking a dispensation, rather than as a cause excusing the candidate from the payment of the dowry; cf. Jardi, *El Derecho de las Religiosas,* p. 170, n. 454; Coronata, *Institutiones,* I, p. 725, n. 577, c), and footnote 5.

[32] Cf. canon 569, § 1.

the monastery.[33]   On the other hand, if the excess is intended by the donor to remain as an integral part of her own dowry, the superioress who would apply it in favor of another postulant would act contrary to the prescription of canon 549, which forbids the disposal of the dowry before the death of the religious who brought it.[34]   The candidate who freely consented to the application of the excess of her dowry in favor of another candidate thereby relinquishes all claim to the money and cannot recover it if she leaves the institute.[35]   On the other hand, the institute is obliged to restore it to the religious in whose favor it was given if she leaves the community.[36]

In the above and similar instances, although the postulant herself is unable to pay the dowry, the entire amount is supplied from another source, with the institute receiving full value. Any plan of payment, however, which entails even a partial condonation of the dowry is forbidden without a dispensation from the proper ecclesiastical authority named in canon 547, § 4.

Different somewhat from the plan whereby the regular amount of the dowry is paid by another person in favor of a candidate is the case of endowments wherein a capital sum is invested and assigned to a candidate as her dowry. For example, a benefactor may, under the condition that his bequest be assigned to a girl who is unable to pay the dowry, bequeath $200.00 to a religious congregation in which the requisite dowry is established at $100.00. According to this arrangement the capital sum of the bequest is not returned in the event of her departure to the one for whom it served as a dowry, nor is it acquired by the institute in the event of her death upon continued membership in the institute, but in either event it is successively credited to a new candidate for whom it is to serve as the requisite dowry. Such a plan is not contemplated in the Code, but it is permitted, especially if, as authors assert, the capital thus assigned to a religious is consider-

---

[33] Cf. Bastien, *Directoire canonique* (1923), p. 65, n. 100.

[34] Cf. Fanfani, *De Iure Religiosorum*, p. 189, n. 168, dubium II.

[35] Cf. Schaefer, *op. cit.*, p. 503, n. 228; Fanfani, *op. cit.*, p. 192, n. 172, dubium I; Gerster, *op. cit.*, p. 86.

[36] Cf. Fanfani, *op. cit.*, p. 189, n. 168, dubium II, and p. 192, n. 172; Beste, *Introductio in Codicem*, p. 367.

ably larger than the customary dowry. The precise quantity cannot be stated with mathematical exactness, but some authors say it should be double the prescribed amount.[37] The income earned by that portion of the bequest which is in excess of the requisite dowry will thus compensate for the financial loss resulting from the fact that the religious institute never acquires the original capital.[38] Any arrangement, however, whereby this compensation is lacking is equivalent to a condonation and is consequently forbidden unless it be granted by the Holy See for pontifical institutes, or by the local ordinary for diocesan institutes.[39]

This manner of payment of the dowry involves a procedure somewhat at variance with that of the Code. For example, the law requires that the payment of the dowry, or at least its guarantee, be made to the monastery before the reception of the habit;[40] that the dowry be irrevocably acquired by the monastery on the death of the religious;[41] that the dowry be invested after the first profession;[42] and that it be restored to the religious who for any reason departs.[43] Accurate compliance with these prescriptions is not possible when dowries are assigned successively from endowments.

The most serious objection to the plan lies in the difficulties which arise when a religious leaves the institute. From the intention of the founder the endowment is given directly in favor of the monastery and is destined for the support of the professed religious. It is not his intention, unless expressly indicated, that the money should ever be acquired by the person in whose favor the endowment was assigned.[44] Under such arrangement the law

---

[37] Cf. Schaefer, *De Religiosis,* p. 503, n. 228; Jardi, *El Derecho de las Religiosas,* p. 171, n. 454, d) ; Wernz-Vidal, *De Religiosis,* p. 224, n. 268 and footnote 18; Goyeneche, "Consultationes,"—*CpRM,* XI (1930), 36; cf. also Blat, *Commentarium,* II, p. 313, n. 326.

[38] Cf. Jardi, *loc. cit.*

[39] Cf. Schaefer, *loc. cit.;* Goyeneche, *loc. cit.*

[40] Canon 547, § 2.

[41] Canon 548.

[42] Canon 549.

[43] Canon 551, § 1.

[44] Cf. Wernz-Vidal, *op. cit.,* p. 224, footnote 18; Creusen-Garesché-Ellis, *Religious Men and Women in the Code,* p. 145, n. 187.

of canon 551, § 1, becomes difficult to observe. This canon imposes the obligation on the institute of *restoring* the capital of the dowry to a religious who for any reason leaves the community. But, since upon her entrance she *gave* nothing, therefore strictly considered nothing can be *restored* to her.[45] Nevertheless, the intention of the legislator in requiring the restoration of the dowry, that is, to furnish a respectable living for the departing religious, is provided for by the law of canon 643, § 2. This canon states that if a woman was received without a dowry and cannot provide for herself out of her own goods after her departure, the institute must give her sufficient funds to insure a decent living for a time to be fixed by mutual agreement. Under the endowment plan of dowries, the community will be able to supply the necessary funds from the income received on that part of the capital of the endowment which is in excess of the required dowry; and thus the purpose of canons 551, § 1, and 643, § 2, is fulfilled. Support is given to this solution by a reply of the Sacred Congregation of Religious on March 2, 1924. The Sacred Congregation stated that a religious institute in which the dowry does not amount to as much as the reasonably estimated charitable subsidy is not relieved of all obligation toward the departing religious by the mere restitution of her dowry, but on the contrary the institute is bound to supply the amount which is wanting to make up a fitting charitable subsidy according to canon 643, § 2.[46]

------

[45] Cf. Wernz-Vidal, *loc. cit.;* Creusen-Garesché-Ellis, *loc. cit.*

[46] Cf. *AAS,* XVI (1924), 165; Wernz-Vidal, *loc. cit.;* Creusen-Garesché-Ellis, *loc. cit.*

CHAPTER VIII

Investment of the Dowry

Canon 549: Post primam religiosae professionem dos in tutis, licitis ac fructiferis nominibus collocetur ab Antistita cum suo Consilio, de consensu Ordinarii loci et Superioris regularis, si domus ab hoc dependeat; . . .

Having thus far treated the legislation dealing with questions involved up to the time the religious institute acquires actual possession of the funds given in payment of the dowry, one must now give consideration to the canonical prescriptions pertaining to the care of these funds after they have been paid to the institute. Canon 549, which prescribes that the dowries be placed in safe, lawful and productive investments, follows as a natural consequence of the primary purpose of the dowry. As stated frequently in the present work, the principal end of the dowry is to provide a means of support for the professed religious. This support is derived, not from the capital sum paid by the candidate—for this must remain intact during her life in the community—but from the income earned through the investment of that capital. For the twofold purpose of safeguarding the dotal funds and of assuring a reasonable income from them, special prescriptions are given in canons 549 and 550 governing the investment and administration of the dowries. These prescriptions apply to all types of religious institutes of women in which a dowry is paid by the candidates.

Canon 549 states that after the first profession of a religious her dowry shall be invested in safe, lawful and productive securities by the superioress with her council and with the consent of the local ordinary and, if the house is subject to regulars, of the regular superior. Three principal elements are noted in the prescription of this canon: 1) The time for making the invest-

81

ment; 2) the type of investment; 3) the persons authorized to make the investment.

Canon 549 prescribes that the dowry be invested after the first profession of the religious. The profession here mentioned is that which follows immediately after the completion of the novitiate.[1] Regardless of the type of religious institutes in which this profession is made, it is always of a temporary character.[2] The privilege granted by the Holy See for a novice to make profession at the point of death produces only spiritual effects, and therefore such profession is not to be taken into consideration in regard to the investment and administration of the dowry.[3]

In stating that the dowry must be invested after the first profession of the religious, the Code establishes the time at which the obligation of investing the dowry begins, but it refrains from determining a definite period within which the obligation must be fulfilled. From the moment of the first profession of the religious the institute has the right to the income from the invested dowry. If those whose duty it is to make the investment delay beyond a reasonable limit, they are unjustly depriving the institute of the corresponding income. On the other hand, sufficient time should be taken to insure a safe, lawful and productive investment in accordance with the prescription of canon 549. It may easily happen that at times a delay be unavoidable in finding a suitable investment. It suffices to say that the investment should be made as soon after the first profession of the religious as it can be done properly and legitimately.[4]

Although the Code states that the dowry should be invested after the first profession, the doubt arises as to whether or not it is permitted to make the investment before that time. There is no question here of a simple deposit of the money in a bank for

---

[1] Cf. Blat, *Commentarium*, II, p. 315, n. 334.

[2] Cf. canon 574.

[3] Cf. S. C. de Rel., 30 dec. 1922—*AAS*, XV (1922), 156-158.

[4] Schaefer, *De Religiosis*, p. 504, n. 229; Goyeneche, "Consultationes,"— *CpRM*, XI (1930), 38.

securing the funds and facilitating the performance of financial transactions, but rather of an investment properly so called, wherein the money is exchanged for securities with a view of obtaining an income or profit. Some authors affirm that the dowry may be invested while the person is still a postulant or a novice if her permission is obtained, and also the permission of her parents if she is still subject to them.[5] Bastien[6] and Vermeersch-Creusen[7] imply that the investment is sometimes made before profession when they state that the dowry should be invested after the first profession of the candidate if it has not been done before. Similarly, those authors who permit the acceptance of securities and other productive goods in place of money as payment of the dowry admit by this very fact that the investment may be made before the profession of the candidate.[8] In these cases, however, the securities should possess the qualities required by canon 549, and should be acceptable to those persons whose duty it is to make and pass judgment on the investments, that is, to the superioress, her council, the local ordinary, and the religious superior to whom the community may be subject.

Larraona denies that the dowry may be invested during the novitiate. Such a practice, he says, is full of dangers and is contrary to the historical evolution of the dowry; furthermore, the income derived from these improper investments does not belong to the religious institute, for during the time that a person continues as a postulant or as a novice only that reimbursement which is permitted according to the norm of canon 570, § 1, can be claimed by the institute. This reimbursement, if it be demanded by the constitutions or in view of an express agreement between the institute and the entrant, implies the making of some payment towards compensating the institute for its incurred expense in providing the candidate with her sustenance and religious habit.[9]

---

[5] Schaefer, *op. cit.,* p. 505, n. 229; Gerster, *Ius Religiosorum,* p. 87; Fanfani, *De Iure Religiosorum,* p. 190, n. 169.

[6] *Directoire canonique* (1923), p. 66, n. 101.

[7] *Epitome,* I, p. 499, n. 699.

[8] Cf. *supra,* p. 60.

[9] "Commentarium Codicis,"—*CpRM,* XXI (1940), 28, footnote 732, and XX (1939), 13, footnote 609; cf. Fuchs, Rückgabe der Mitgift an die

In prescribing that the dowry be invested after the first profession, the wording of canon 549 does not directly forbid the making of the investment before that time. Nevertheless, since the candidate is only on probation and is still free to leave or to be dismissed, the very nature of this unstable relationship argues against the advisability of a premature investment of the dowry, particularly in securities of a relatively long term. However, this does not necessarily eliminate the possibility of investing the dowry during the novitiate, especially if an opportunity of an attractive investment arises which would not be available after the profession of the candidate. In such a case there would seem to be no objection to the making of the investment provided the candidate and, if she is still a minor, her parents or guardians consented,[10] and provided, further, that the other prescriptions of law pertaining to the investment be complied with.

ARTICLE II. THE TYPE OF INVESTMENT

The Code introduces a change in the law regarding the type of investment for the dowries. Formerly it was required that the money be invested in immovable goods or real estate (*bona stabilia*),[11] because this type of investment was considered the safer and more secure kind of investment.[12] Now, however, the law specifically states that the dowry shall be invested in securities (*in nominibus*).[13] These are preferred on account of the greater danger of confiscation relative to immovable property and on account of the difficulties involved in administering it.[14] By

---

ausscheidende Klosterfrau,"—*ThPrQs*, LXXXVIII (1935), 362. Schaefer (*op. cit.*, p. 504, n. 229) says this income belongs to the institute.

[10] Cf. Schaefer, *op. cit.*, p. 505, n. 229; Gerster, *loc. cit.*; Fanfani, *loc. cit.*

[11] S. C. Ep. et Reg., *Portugalien.*, 6 iunii 1615—*Fontes*, n. 1666; *Senen.*, 17 febr. 1645—*Fontes*, n. 1772; *Assisien.*, 4 oct. 1823—*Fontes*, n. 1898; S. C. Ep. et Reg., 24 nov. 1780—Lucidi, *De Visitatione*, vol. II, c. V, § 5, n. 191.

[12] Larraona, "Commentarium Codicis,"—*CpRM*, XXI (1940), 30.

[13] Canon 549.

[14] Cf. Larraona, "Commentarium Codicis,"—*CpRM*, XII (1931), 436, footnote 502; McManus, *The Administration of Temporal Goods in Religious Institutes,* The Catholic University of America, Canon Law Studies, n. 109 (Washington, D. C.: The Catholic University of America, 1937), 93.

limiting the investment to securities the Code imposes a sound, uniform and conservative financial policy which better guarantees an efficient and successful administration of the dowry.

Notwithstanding the precise wording of the Code in restricting the investment to securities, some authors, who permit the dowry to be paid in the form of immovable goods instead of money, also permit the community to retain those goods or that property as an invested dowry, provided that they constitute a safe, lawful and productive investment.[15] Jombart[16] and Wernz-Vidal[17] even permit the dowry which is paid in money to be invested in real estate. It is difficult to reconcile with the wording of the Code those opinions which allow the dowry to be retained in the form of real estate or to be invested in any form of immovable goods. Canon 549 orders the investment to be made in "securities," which term does not include real estate.[18] Oesterle observes that securities are preferred to immovable goods for practical reasons, for example, because of the convenience in restoring the dowry in the case of the departure of a religious. He adds that the practice of the Roman Curia demands that the investment be made in securities.[19]

A convincing argument in favor of the necessity of investing the dowry in securities to the exclusion of other types of investment is found in the modification of the wording of the preliminary text of the Code in the present law. In the drafted text of 1914 and 1916 the wording was as follows: "Post religiosae profes-sionem dos in tuto, licito ac fructifero investimento collocetur. . . ." The law as contained in canon 549 reads: "Post primam religiosae professionem dos in tutis, licitis ac fructiferis *nominibus* collocetur.

---

[15] Cappello, *Summa,* II, p. 203, n. 604; Bastien, *Directoire canonique* (1923), p. 66, n. 101; Jombart, "Une dot qui consisterait en une maison,"— *Revue des communautés religieuses,* I (1925), 158.

[16] *Loc. cit.;* this author admits, however, that the investment of the dowries in real estate has its disadvantages and should be advised only in exceptional cases.

[17] *De Religiosis,* p. 222, footnote 14.

[18] Cf. Larraona, "Commentarium Codicis,"—*CpRM,* XX (1939), 15, and XXI (1940), 28. Wernz-Vidal (*loc. cit.*) say it is not apparent why real estate is not equivalent to securities in the sense of this canon.

[19] *Praelectiones Iuris Canonici,* I, 301.

. . ." The substitution of the word *"nominibus"* unquestionably indicates that the legislator intended to restrict the investment of dowries to a particular type of investments, that is, to securities. In view of the clear declaration of the law it is difficult to justify the resort to other types of investment, as Vermeersch-Creusen allow by the use of *epikeia,*[20] even though it may be true, as these authors state, that at the present time investments in securities are frequently dangerous.[21] This danger, however, was recognized by the legislator when he imposed the obligation on the investors of the dowry to choose "safe, lawful and productive" investments.[22] Strict adherence to this norm insofar as diligent care, practical experience and prudent judgment allow will reduce to a minimum the danger of loss in the selection of investments which correspond to the type specified by law. In the event that securities which measure up to the required qualities cannot be found, then it seems that recourse must be had to the Holy See for permission to make other types of investment.[23] The local ordinary does not possess the authority to grant a dispensation from the common law in this matter, even for diocesan institutes, except in accordance with the norm of canon 81.

Chief among the securities included in the term *"nomina"* are stocks, bonds and mortgages, all of which are a common and popular form of investment.[24] Stocks consist in securities by which the purchaser becomes a stockholder in a corporation. The income from this form of investment is derived from the profits of the corporation, and therefore is somewhat precarious as well as variable, depending on the degree of the success of the enterprise. Bonds correspond to a secured loan at a definite rate of interest, and are issued by the government and subdivisions thereof,

---

[20] *Epitome,* I, p. 499, n. 699: "Cum imperata collocatio in nominibus hodie non raro facta sit periculosa, nonne consentiente Ordinario cum Superiorissa, aliam collocationem fructuosam et magis tutam eligere licebit? Ita ex rationabili epikeia fieri posse, immo interdum debere censemus."

[21] Cf. Larraona, "Commentarium Codicis,"—*CpRM,* XXI (1940), 29.

[22] Cf. canon 549.

[23] Cf. Larraona, *loc. cit.*

[24] Kiekhofer, *Economic Principles, Problems and Policies* (New York: Appleton-Century, 1936), p. 685.

corporations, institutions, etc. As a general rule the larger profits derived from stocks than from bonds is offset by the greater element of risk in the former.

Whatever form of security is selected it must have the three qualities demanded by canon 549, that is, it must be safe, lawful and productive.[25]

Safe—Safety stands out as the primary consideration in selecting a suitable investment, because the preservation of the capital is of more primary importance than a return of interest or an accruing of income. In fact, if through imprudent investing the capital is lost or diminished, the earned income suffers a corresponding fate. Consequently, a safe investment which nets a small but fully assured rate of interest is preferred to a less secure investment which gives promise of a greater but at the same time less reliably certified return in interest. Diligent care combined with good business judgment on the part of the superioress, her council, the local ordinary and the regular superior, will help to safeguard the dowries and reduce to a minimum the element of risk which is present in every investment.

Lawful—The investment must be lawful from the standpoint of the nature of the business and the manner in which it is conducted.[26] For example, investing the dowry in a gambling house or anti-Catholic society would be unlawful. Furthermore, the investment must be such that it does not involve the violation of other laws, especially those which prohibit clerics and religious from engaging in commercial enterprises. Canon 142 forbids clerics to engage either personally or through others in any business or trading, whether for their own benefit or for that of others. And canon 592 extends this prohibition to all religious. Therefore, in the investment of dowries the investors must avoid transactions forbidden by the above laws. According to canon 2380 clerics or religious who, either in person or through others, engage in trading and business in violation of the precept of canon 142 shall be punished by the ordinary with appropriate penalties in proportion to the gravity of their guilt.

---

[25] The *Normae* of 1901 (art. 94) contained a similar prescription: "Tradita dos alienari non potest, sed probe, tuto ac fructuose collocari debet."

[26] Blat, *Commentarium*, II, p. 315, n. 334.

Strict commercial trading (*negotiatio lucrativa seu quaestuosa*), which is defined as the buying of things with the intention of selling them unchanged at a higher price, and strict artificial trading (*negotiatio artificialis seu industrialis*), which consists in the buying of material with the intention of changing it by means of hired labor and of selling the article at a profit, are the two principal forms of trading which have been forbidden to clerics by the Church throughout the centuries.[27]

The former uncertainty concerning the lawfulness for clerics to purchase stocks in companies which engage in forms of trading forbidden to clerics no longer exists. The common opinion today maintains that clerics may purchase stocks in all forms of companies which pursue a lawful commercial or industrial enterprise with the employment of lawful business methods.[28] Although stockholders become part owners of the company, they have only a remote participation in the business.

Productive—If the dowry is to serve the full purpose which is contemplated for it, then the capital must be placed in a productive investment, in order that the consequent income may contribute to the support of the professed religious. No uniform rule can be given to determine the rate or percentage of interest that should be obtained. This is a relative and variable quantity, which depends on general financial conditions as well as on various other circumstances. As a general rule the percentage of income is in inverse ratio to the safety of the investment. While searching for profitable securities the investors of the dowries should always keep in mind that safety is the primary consideration.

Those charged with the duty of investing the dowry enjoy full freedom in apportioning the money among the investments selected. That is, each single dowry may retain its identity and be invested as an independent unit, or the capital representing several dowries may be merged into a single investment with a

---

[27] Brunini, *The Clerical Obligations of Canons 139 and 142*, The Catholic University of America, Canon Law Studies, n. 103 (Washington, D. C.: The Catholic University of America, 1937), pp. 77-78; cf. Battandier, *Guide canonique* (1923), pp. 146-147, n. 177.

[28] Cf. Brunini, *op. cit.,* p. 101, and authors there cited.

proportionate share assigned to each dowry.[29] The method selected assumes a practical importance in the determination of the precise amount to be restored to a candidate in the event she leaves the community.[30]

ARTICLE III. THE PERSONS AUTHORIZED TO MAKE THE INVESTMENT

Canon 549 prescribes that the dowry be invested by the superioress with her council, and with the consent of the local ordinary, and also of the regular superior in the event of the jurisdictional subjection of the religious house to regulars. Therefore, the following persons participate in one way or another in the investment of the dowry: The superioress, her council, the local ordinary, and sometimes a regular superior. Not all, however, have the same voice or equal power, as is evident from the above canon, which states briefly the rights of each in the responsible task of placing the dowries in suitable investments.

In monasteries of nuns the superioress referred to in this canon is the superioress of the house, while in congregations of sisters she is the general or provincial superioress in accordance with the norm of canon 550, § 1, and the regulation of the particular constitutions.[31] The council mentioned in canon 549 is determined by the same norm as the superioress and therefore is the council of the monastery, or the general or provincial council, depending on the type of institute.[32]

The power of making the investment rests primarily with the religious superioress, but there are certain restrictions placed upon the exercise of her power. In the first place she must act "with her council" (*cum suo consilio*). This clause indicates

---

[29] Cf. Creusen-Garesché-Ellis, *Reliigous Men and Women in the Code*, pp. 144-145, n. 186; Jombart, "Les dots,"—*Revue des Communautés Religieuses,* III (1927), 55.

[30] Cf. *infra,* pp. 117-118.

[31] Cf. Blat, *Commentarium,* II, p. 316, n. 335; Coronata, *Institutiones,* I, p. 727, n. 577; Bastien, *Directoire canonique* (1923), p. 66, n. 101; Vromant, *De Bonis Ecclesiae Temporalibus,* p. 269, n. 255.

[32] Coronata, *loc. cit.*

that the superioress is bound to obtain the consultative vote of her council.[33] Particular constitutions, however, frequently impose the necessity of a decisive vote of the council for the investment of dowries.[34]

The second restriction placed on the power of the superioress in investing the dowry is the law which requires her to obtain the consent of the local ordinary and, if the house is subject to regulars, of the regular superior.[35]

Few authors discuss the problem of whether the consent of the local ordinary, and likewise that of the regular superior, is necessary for the validity of the investment by the superioress. Vromant[36] and McManus[37] affirm that the consent is necessary only for the licitness of the act, while Toso[38] and Larraona[39] maintain with apparently stronger reason that this consent is necessary also for the validity of the act. Canon 549 clearly requires the superioress to seek the consent of the local ordinary and also of the regular superior if the house is subject to regulars.

---

[33] Cf. Vermeersch-Creusen, *Epitome,* I, p. 499, n. 699; Coronata, *Institutiones,* I, p. 727, n. 577; Wernz-Vidal, *De Religiosis,* p. 225, n. 269; Vromant, *De Bonis Ecclesiae Temporalibus,* p. 269, n. 255; Toso, *Commentaria,* lib. II, pars II, p. 110; Oesterle, *Praelectiones Iuris Canonici,* I, 301; Raus, *Institutiones Canonicae,* p. 301, n. 186; Cocchi, *Commentarium,* IV, p. 143, n. 67; Larraona, "Commentarium Codicis,"—*CpRM,* XXI (1940), 31-32; Schaefer, *De Religiosis,* p. 505, n. 229. Blat (*Commentarium,* II, p. 316, n. 335) holds that a decisive vote is necessary, and Schaefer held the same opinion in a previous edition (1927, p. 288, n. 229).

[34] Cf. Larraona, "Commentarium Codicis,"—*CpRM,* XXI (1940), 32.

[35] Cf. canon 549.

[36] *De Bonis Ecclesiae Temporalibus,* p. 269, n. 255.

[37] *The Administration of Temporal Goods in Religious Institutes,* p. 93.

[38] *Commentaria,* lib. II, pars II, p. 110, n. 2.

[39] "Commentarium Codicis,"—*CpRM,* XXI (1940), 32. This author formerly held, in his commentary on canon 533, § 1, that the consent of the local ordinary which the superioresses of nuns and of diocesan congregations needed to have for effecting the specific investment of the money (including the dowries) of their monastery or institute, and which consent the superioresses of pontifical institutes needed to have for effecting the specific investment of the dowries of their institute, was required for the lawfulness but not for the validity of the act—cf. "Commentarium Codicis,"— *CpRM,* XII (1931), 439-440.

And canon 105, n. 1, states that whenever the law requires the superior to seek the consent of some persons before acting, any action contrary to the vote or decision of these persons is invalid. Therefore, it follows that the superioress who invests the dowry without obtaining the consent of the local ordinary—and when necessary, the consent of the regular superior—enters into an illicit and invalid investment contract. Only the Holy See can rectify the nullifying defect without repeating the formalities prescribed by the law for investing the dowries. The ordinary or regular superior whose consent was neglected are incompetent to grant a sanation to heal the original act of investment. The reason for their incompetency lies in the fact that such a ratification amounts to a dispensation from the formality prescribed by the supreme legislator.[40] In the meantime, the institute has full right to the income from the invested dowry even though the investment contract is canonically invalid. No one other than the institute itself has any title by which that income can be claimed. Furthermore, the rights of the community to such income are given additional legal protection by the principle enunciated in canon 1527, § 2, which states that an ecclesiastical legal person[41] is not liable for contracts made by administrators who act without obtaining the permission of the competent superior, except when and insofar as the contracts are favorable to the legal person.

It must be noted, however, that the local ordinary does not have the power or authority to choose the investment. He merely passes judgment on the preliminary choice proposed by the religious superioress. If in his judgment the contemplated investment is safe, lawful and productive he is obliged to give his consent. If he judges the investment to be lacking in any of these qualities his right is limited to the withholding of his consent until the choice of a satisfactory investment is proposed by the religious superioress. Under no circumstance can he

---

[40] Cf. S. C. C., *Albinganen. et Aliarum,* 17 maii 1919—*AAS,* XI (1919), 382-387; cf. also Vromant, *De Bonis Ecclesiae Temporalibus,* p. 311, n. 295.
[41] Cf. canon 1498.

himself assume the right to choose the investment.[42] The same rules apply to the regular superior if the house is subject to regulars. If these persons, that is, the superioress, the local ordinary and when necessary the regular superior cannot come to a unanimous agreement on a satisfactory investment, then the matter must be referred to the Holy See.[43]

The Code does not specify the manner in which the consent of the local ordinary and the regular superior shall be given. Therefore, they may give their permission either in each single case, or in more or less general terms, such as by approving a certain type of securities, or by granting approval on the fulfillment of certain conditions.[44]

The consent of the local ordinary and of the regular superior, as required by canon 549 applies exclusively to the investment of the money contributed to the community in payment of the dowry of the candidates. Canon 533, § 1, likewise demands the consent of these persons, not only for the investment of the dowries, but in some cases for other investments as well. This canon provides that in the investment of money the particular constitutions are to be followed, as is prescribed in canon 532; but the previous consent of the local ordinary must be obtained by the following: 1) The superioresses of nuns and of diocesan congregations for every investment of money (therefore, including the dowry); if the monastery of nuns is subject to a regular superior, his consent is also necessary; 2) the superioresses in pontifical institutes, if the money to be invested is the dowry of professed sisters, according to the norm of canon 549. Canon 533, § 2, requires that these rules must likewise be observed for every change of the investment.

---

[42] Cf. Coronata, *Institutiones,* I, p. 726, n. 577; Larraona, "Commentarium Codicis,"—*CpRM,* XXI (1940), 33; Bastien, *Directoire canonique* (1923), p. 66, n. 101.

[43] Vermeersch-Creusen, *Epitome,* I, p. 499, n. 699; Coronata, *op. cit.,* p. 727, n. 577; Bastien, *loc. cit.;* Larraona, *loc. cit.*

[44] Cf. Larraona, "Commentarium Codicis,"—*CpRM,* XII (1931), 439; Oesterle, *Praelectiones Iuris Canonici,* I, 277; Coronata, *loc. cit.*

Canon 549: . . . ; omnino autem prohibetur eam [i.e., dotem] quoquo modo ante religiosae obitum impendi, ne ad aedificandam quidem domum aut ad aes alienum extinguendum.

Closely allied with the law concerning the investment of the dowry is the latter part of canon 549 which forbids the expenditure of the capital sum before the death of the religious. It cannot be spent for any purpose whatsoever, not even for the erection of buildings or for the payment of the debts of the community. This law of the Code restates the strict rule which has long been in force to insure the preservation of the dowry during the lifetime of the religious.[45] The prohibition to dispose of the dowry is logical and reasonable in view of the fact that the community does not acquire complete and irrevocable title to it until the death of the professed religious.[46] The investment and conservation of the capital of the dowry are necessary for the fulfillment of the two closely linked purposes of the dowry: first, to provide a means of support for the professed religious during her life in the community, and, secondly, to supply her with a decent livelihood if she departs or is dismissed from the institute.

If, on account of extremely grave circumstances, the alienation of even one dowry is judged necessary, permission must be obtained from the Holy See.[47] The Sacred Congregation, in granting this permission, imposes the obligation of restoring the amount thus legitimately alienated.[48]

The prohibition to alienate the dowry is fortified by a penal sanction in canon 2412, n. 1. The superioresses of all women religious, even of exempt organizations, shall be punished by the

---

[45] Cf. *supra*, pp. 33-34.

[46] Cf. canon 548.

[47] Cf. inst. *"Inter Ea,"* S. C. de Rel., 30 iulii 1909, art. 12—*Fontes,* n. 4394; Battandier, *Guide canonique* (1923), p. 145, n. 176; Bastien, *Directoire canonique* (1923), p. 67, n. 102.

[48] Cf. Schaefer, *De Religiosis,* p. 505, n. 229; Larraona, "Commentarium Codicis,"—*CpRM,* XXI (1940), 35; Bastien, *loc. cit.;* Gerster, *Ius Religiosorum,* p. 87.

local ordinary in proportion to the gravity of their guilt, not excluding deprivation of office if, in violation of the precept of canon 549, they presume to expend in any manner the dowries of the young women who have been received into the community; furthermore, if the dowry of a religious was thus unlawfully alienated, the obligation remains of restoring it to her if she leaves the community or transfers to another institute.[49]

---

[49] Cf. canon 551.

CHAPTER IX

Administration of the Dowry

Article I. Duties of the Superioress

Canon 550, § 1: Dotes caute et integre administrentur apud monasterium vel domum habitualis residentiae supremae Moderatricis aut Antistitae provincialis.

The investment of the dowry and the prohibition to divert the capital sum from its intended purpose to any other purpose whatsoever, both of which points were treated in the preceding chapter, are not distinct from the administration of these funds, but rather constitute a part of it. The present chapter is concerned with a consideration of the other prescriptions of law, especially of those which are contained in canons 550 and 535, as touching upon the administration of dowries.

Canon 550, § 1, contains a note of caution on the manner of administering the dowries, and also establishes the rule for determining the place in which the acts of administration are to be performed. "The dowries must be administered carefully and integrally at the monastery or house of the habitual residence of the general or provincial superioress."

By the administration of temporal goods, which include the dowry, is meant the proper care which is to be exercised relative to these goods according to their nature and purpose.[1] It embraces all acts which are necessary or useful for the preservation and improvement of the goods, for making them productive, for collecting the income, and for properly applying the goods and income according to their purpose.[2] If the dowry is to achieve

---

[1] Vermeersch-Creusen, *Epitome,* I, p. 469, n. 651; Wernz-Vidal, *De Religiosis,* p. 171, n. 218.

[2] Vermeersch-Creusen, *loc. cit.;* Wernz-Vidal, *loc. cit.;* Vromant, *De Bonis Ecclesiae Temporalibus,* p. 184, n. 172; Schaefer, *Re Religiosis,* p.

the ends for which it exists, it is evident that the acts of administration must be performed carefully and integrally as canon 550, § 1, demands. The administrators must act *carefully,* that is, with circumspection and prudence in the discharge of their duty in order to guard against the danger of loss or diminution of the funds. Carelessness in preserving the principal, imprudence in investing it, negligence in collecting the income, and disregard of civil laws pertaining to investments and securities, are some of the abuses that can easily result in serious detriment to the institute, to the religious, or to both. Particular constitutions often supplement the general law by prescribing more detailed rules to be observed in the administration of the dowries. In virtue of canon 532 religious administrators are bound to adhere to these norms. They should remember that they are not the owners, but only the administrators of the funds committed to their care.[3]

Administrators are also bound to administer the dowries *integrally,* that is, the exercise of their duty of administration must extend to the entire amount of money, securities, interest, etc., which in any way pertain to the dowry.[4] The obligation of administering the dowries carefully and integrally extends to all religious institutes wherein a dowry is paid by the postulants. The nature of the vows or the type of institute makes no difference.

The second part of canon 550, § 1, establishes the place wherein the work of administration of the dowries must be conducted. For the purpose of explaining this law, institutes of women religious may be divided into two classes: first, monasteries of nuns with solemn vows, and, secondly, all other religious institutes. In the former, the individual house constitutes a complete juridical entity independent of all other houses. It is consequently fully autonomous (*sui juris*). Canon 550, § 1, prescribes that in

---

415, n. 192; Larraona, "Commentarium Codicis,"—*CpRM,* XII (1931), 355-356; Fanfani, *De Iure Religiosorum,* p. 171, n. 155.

[3] Pruemmer, *Manuale Iuris Canonici,* p. 261, q. 195.

[4] Cocchi, *Commentarium,* IV, p. 143, n. 67; Blat, *Commentarium,* II, p. 317, n. 339.

this type of religious institute the dowries be administered in the house itself. The obligation rests on the superioress, but she may delegate the work to some other religious within the house, not, however, to an outside person.

In the case of the other types of religious institutes the Code allows a measure of freedom to be more accurately determined by the particular constitutions. In all congregations, including both pontifical and diocesan institutes, the dowries are to be administered at the house of the habitual residence of the general or provincial superioress.[5] If the institute is not divided into provinces it has no choice in the matter of the place in which the dowries are to be administered. And it matters not whether the institute consists of one or of many houses, the work must be carried on at the house of the habitual residence of the general superioress. On the other hand, when an institute is divided into provinces, the Code imposes the obligation of administering the dowries at the house of the habitual residence of either the general or the provincial superioress. The determination of one or the other is left to the constitutions.[6] It should be noted, however, that the Code expressly demands that the administration be conducted at the *habitual* residence of the proper superioress. This restriction confines the administration of the dowries to the general house or the provincial houses of the institute, to the exclusion of local houses as well as any other place where the superioress may perchance have a temporary residence.[7] In the event that the constitutions do not determine which of the acceptable places shall be the seat of the administration of the dowries, the right to make this determination rests with the general superioress with her council. As long as the prescriptions of the general law are complied with the administration of the dowries may be divided, that is, it may be conceded to some provinces, while for others it may be conducted at the house of the general superioress.[8] In fact, circumstances may some-

---

[5] Canon 550, § 1.

[6] Cf. Blat, *op. cit.*, II, p. 318, n. 339.

[7] Cf. DeMeester, *Compendium*, II, 437; Vermeersch-Creusen, *Epitome*, I, pp. 498-499, n. 699; Bastien, *Directoire canonique* (1923), p. 67, n. 103.

[8] Larraona, "Commentarium Codicis,"—*CpRM*, XXI (1940), 81.

times urge this division, for example, when some provinces are comparatively small, or when the general house is overburdened with the care of an excessive number of dowries.

Although the Code leaves the institute entirely free to decide whether the administration of the dowries be centralized at the house of the general superioress or committed to the various provincial houses, authors advise that in practice it is safer and usually preferable to allow the provincial superioresses to have charge of the work.[9]

The Code does not commit the care of the dowries to the personal charge of the general or provincial superioress, but rather to the *house*. The work may be delegated to some other member of the community under the supervision of the respective superioress. It is evident that the accounts of the dotal funds should be kept distinct from the other accounts of the house. This is especially necessary in order that the proper report of the administration of the dowries may be made to the local ordinary as prescribed by canon 535, §§ 1-2.

ARTICLE II. VIGILANCE OF THE LOCAL ORDINARY

Canon 550, § 2: Ordinarii locorum conservandis religiosarum dotibus sedulo invigilent; et praesertim in sacra visitatione de eisdem rationem exigant.

Canon 550, § 2, confers on the local ordinary the right and the duty of exercising a diligent vigilance over the dowries in order that these funds may be properly conserved. His power of vigilance differs from, and should not be confused with, the power of administration possessed by the religious superioresses. The right of vigilance over the dowries authorizes the local ordinary to see that all the prescriptions of law are complied with in the administration of these funds. It includes the right to demand an accounting of the funds, to see that the money is

---

[9] Cf. Battandier, *Guide canonique* (1923), p. 146, n. 177; Vromant, *De Bonis Ecclesiae Temporalibus*, p. 269, n. 255; Creusen-Garesché-Ellis, *Religious Men and Women in the Code*, p. 145, n. 186.

invested in safe, lawful and productive securities by the superioress after having obtained his consent, and to see that the money and securities are properly conserved and not spent even for the erection of buildings or for the payment of the debts of the community.[10] These powers of the local ordinary do not give him the right to administer the goods, but only to see to their proper administration by those who, according to the prescriptions of the general and particular law, are endowed with that power. Canon 618, § 2, n. 1, expressly forbids the local ordinary to interfere with the economic affairs of pontifical institutes beyond the limits permitted him in canons 533-535.[11]

ARTICLE III. ACCOUNTS OF THE DOWRIES

Canon 550, § 2, indicates the principal means by which the local ordinary may exercise his power of vigilance over the dowries. He shall demand a financial accounting of the dotal funds, especially at the time of his canonical visitation. Canon 535 contains more specific instructions regarding the financial report to be made by the superioresses to their respective local ordinaries. Since the law for monasteries of nuns is somewhat different from that for other institutes, each will be treated separately.

A. *In Monasteries of Nuns with Solemn Vows*

Canon 535, § 1: In quolibet monialium monasterio etiam exempto:

n. 1. Administrationis ratio, gratis exigenda, reddatur semel in anno, aut etiam saepius si id in constitutionibus praescribatur, ab antistita ordinario loci, itemque superiori regulari, si monasterium sit eidem subiectum;

---

[10] Cf. canons 549 and 550.

[11] These canons deal with the cases wherein it is necessary to obtain the consent of the local ordinary for the investment of money and the alienation of goods and property, and also with those cases in which he has the right to demand a financial accounting from the religious superioresses. Cf. Pruemmer, *Manuale Iuris Canonici,* p. 261, q. 195, n. 4.

The expression "monastery of nuns" (*monialium monasterium*) in this canon includes not only those institutes whose members actually have solemn vows, but also those whose members, in accordance with the direction of the Holy See for certain localities and particular countries, take only simple vows notwithstanding the fact that their constitutions contemplate profession with solemn vows.[12] Furthermore, canon 535, § 1, includes all monasteries of nuns, regardless of the fact whether these monasteries pertain to non-exempt or to exempt religious orders. The superioress is directed to give to the local ordinary a financial report embracing the entire financial administration of the institute. This comprehensive report, therefore, will include an accounting of the administration of the dowries. If the monastery is subject to regulars, the superioress is also obliged to render a similar accounting to the regular superior. This is clear not only from the wording of canon 535, § 1, n. 1, but also from a reply of the Pontifical Commission for the Interpretation of the Code.[13]

According to canon 550, § 2, the local ordinary is bound to demand an account of the dowries from all institutes of women religious, especially at the time of his canonical visitation—every five years.[14] A more specific determination of the time for submitting the report is contained in canon 535, § 1, n. 1, which directs that once a year the superioress of a monastery of nuns must render an accounting of her entire administration (therefore, including the dowries) to the local ordinary and, if the monastery is subject to regulars, to the regular superior. Furthermore, if the constitutions prescribe a more frequent report to be given to the local ordinary, to the regular superior, or to both, these special prescriptions must be followed.[15] Neither the local ordinary nor the regular superior is permitted to demand any remuneration in connection with his task of reviewing this report.

---

[12] Cf. canon 488, n. 7; Toso, *Commentaria,* lib. II, pars II, p. 81, n. 2; Larraona, "Commentarium Codicis,"—*CpRM,* XIV (1933), 345-346.

[13] November 24, 1920—*AAS,* XII (1920), 575.

[14] Cf. canon 512.

[15] Cf. canon 535, § 1, n. 1; Larraona, *ibid.,* 346.

Canon 535, § 1: In quolibet monialium monasterio etiam exempto:

n. 2. Si ratio administrationis Ordinario non probetur, ipse potest opportuna remedia adhibere, etiam removendo, si res postulet, oeconomam aliosque administratores; quod si monasterium sit Superiori regulari subiectum, eum Ordinarius, uti prospiciat, moneat; quod si ille neglexerit, ipse per se consulat.

The local ordinary's right of vigilance over the dowries in monasteries of nuns is strengthened by the power given him in canon 535, § 1, n. 2, whereby he may employ appropriate means to remedy the defect of administration if he does not approve of the report submitted by the superioress. If the case demands it, he may even remove the procurator or other administrators from office. Resort to this severe remedy, however, does not give him the right to appoint a successor to the one removed. Upon the removal from office of the procurator or of some other administrator, a successor would be chosen according to the ordinary norms of the general law and the particular constitutions.

The reasons on account of which the local ordinary does not approve the report need not imply guilt or crime on the part of the administrators. The canon simply says "If the account of the administration is not approved by the ordinary. . . ." Therefore, regardless of the causes for which the report is unsatisfactory, the local ordinary is free to take measures to correct them. A few of the reasons for his disapproval would be: Failure of the superioress to obtain his consent before investing the dowries;[16] the expenditure, without permission from the Holy See, of the capital sum of the dowry before the death of the religious;[17] carelessness and inefficiency in administering the funds;[18] and failure to furnish the prescribed accounting.

The nature of the remedies to be employed are left to the prudent judgment of the local ordinary. He may prescribe what-

---

[16] Cf. canons 533, § 1, n. 1, and 549.
[17] Cf. canons 548 and 549.
[18] Cf. canon 550, § 1.

ever suitable remedies he deems proper for the correction of the unsatisfactory administration. In some cases he may choose merely to offer suggestions or advice, while in others he may find it necessary to inflict penalties on the guilty administrators.[19]

If an unsatisfactory report of the dowries is submitted to the ordinary by a monastery which is subject to a regular superior, the ordinary shall first admonish the superior to take steps to remedy the matter. If the latter neglects to do so, then the ordinary himself has the right to proceed with proper remedies against the administrators of the dowries.

B. *In Other Institutes of Women Religious*

Canon 535, § 2: In aliis mulierum religionibus, ratio administrationis bonorum quae dotes constituunt, Ordinario loci reddatur occasione visitationis et etiam saepius, si Ordinarius id necessarium duxerit.

All pontifical and diocesan institutes of women religious who are not included in the term *moniales*[20] are the object of the law of canon 535, § 2. This law, however, would have no application to those congregations in which a dowry is not prescribed, unless it happened that a postulant paid a sum after the manner of a dowry. In such case the administration of that fund would be subject to the laws on dowry, including the obligation contained in this canon to submit a report to the local ordinary. It may be noted here once again that the Holy See is very reluctant to approve a set of constitutions for a religious congregation of women unless at least a small dowry is prescribed. In the case of monasteries the necessity of a dowry is expressly required by the Code, though the quantity of the dowry is left to be determined by legitimate custom or by the particular constitutions.[21,]

---

[19] Canon 619 states that in all matters in which religious are subject to the local ordinary he may coerce them even by means of penalties.

[20] Cf. canon 488, n. 7.

[21] Cf. canon 547, § 1.

While monasteries of nuns[22] and diocesan institutes of women religious[23] must render an account of their entire financial administration to the local ordinary, pontifical institutes need to render no other account to him than that concerning the funds which constitute the dowries,[24] and the funds given for the special purposes stated in canon 533, § 1, nn. 3-4.[25] Pontifical congregations are responsible directly to the Holy See and therefore enjoy a greater independence from the local ordinary than do diocesan institutes.[26] The former are required to submit a comprehensive quinquennial report to the Holy See, which report, however, must be signed by the ordinary of the diocese or of the archdiocese in which the general superioress and her council reside.[27]

Question 57 of the formula of questions to be answered in this report is: "Have the dowries of the sisters been placed, with the consent of the local ordinary, in safe and profitable investments according to canon law; and has any part of them been used to defray expenses; and, if so, how much, in what manner, and by whose permission?"[28]

From the answers to the various parts of this question the Holy See may judge whether or not the community is properly administering the dowries. In addition to this report to the Holy See each pontifical congregation of women religious must also render an account to the local ordinary. In this matter canon 535, § 2, and canon 550, § 2, are correlative. On the one hand, the former canon states the obligation of the community, be it pontifical or diocesan, to render the account to the local ordinary, while the latter canon states the obligation of the local ordinary to demand it. Both canons prescribe that the account be given on the occasion of the canonical visitation,

---

[22] Cf. canon 535, § 1, n. 1.
[23] Cf. canon 535, § 3, n. 1.
[24] Canon 535, § 2.
[25] Cf. canon 535, § 3, n. 2.
[26] Cf. canon 488, n. 3.
[27] Canon 510.
[28] Bouscaren, *The Canon Law Digest*, I, 288.

that is, every five years,[29] but both also make allowance for a more frequent report. Canon 550, § 2, in requiring the local ordinary to demand the accounting *especially* at the time of his canonical visitation, implies that he may ask for it more often.[30] Canon 535, § 2, is more specific by allowing him to request the accounting of the administration of the dowries more frequently if he thinks it necessary. If, in his prudent judgment he decides that it is necessary for insuring the proper administration of the dowries to demand an account, for example, every two or three years, his ruling is to be followed.

The local ordinary is the only one to whom canon 535, § 2, obliges the institute to give a report. No mention is made of a regular superior, as is the case in the law for monasteries of nuns, because without a special apostolic indult, no religious organization of men can have under its jurisdiction religious congregations of women.[31] In the exceptional cases wherein such jurisdiction exists attention must be given to the provisions of the indult.

The local ordinary whose consent must be obtained for investing the dowries,[32] whose duty of vigilance must be exercised concerning them,[33] and to whom an accounting of these funds must be submitted by the religious community,[34] is not clearly determined by the Code. In the case of independent monasteries there can be no doubt that it is the local ordinary of the territory in which the house is located. In other institutes it seems to be the ordinary of the diocese or archdiocese in which the general house or the respective provincial house is found, depending on which of these two houses is the seat of the administration of the dowries according to canon 550, § 1.[35]

---

[29] Canon 512, § 2, n. 3.

[30] Cf. Bastien, *Directoire canonique* (1923), p. 68, n. 103; Battandier, *Guide canonique* (1923), p. 147, n. 177.

[31] Cf. canon 500, § 3.

[32] Canon 549.

[33] Canon 550, § 2.

[34] Canon 535, §§ 1-2.

[35] Cf. Coronata, *Institutiones*, I, p. 726, n. 577; Blat, *Commentarium*, II, p. 315, n. 334.

The opinion of Pruemmer,[36] followed by Schaefer,[37] that the general or provincial superioress who administers the dowries is obliged to render an account to *each* ordinary in whose territory a house of the community is located seems to be stricter than the law requires. In the first place, those bound to render an account of the dowries are those whose duty it is to administer them. Canon 550, § 1, states that the dowries shall be administered at the house of the habitual residence of the general or provincial superioress. Therefore, the term "local ordinary" should refer to the ordinary of the territory in which the general house or the respective provincial house is located. It would seem to be going beyond the meaning of the words and the intention of the law to require the superioress to give an account to every ordinary in whose diocese is found a house of the community. The local houses of a community have no part in the administration of the funds constituting the dowries of the members stationed there; nor do the respective local ordinaries of such houses have any jurisdiction over the general or provincial superioresses to whom the law commits the administration of the dowries. The ordinary who receives the report is he who has the right of visitation over those who administer the dotal funds.[38] There is no law, however, which gives all local ordinaries in whose territories local houses of a community are established the right to make a canonical visitation of the general or provincial houses located outside of their respective dioceses. The local ordinary's penal power in the case of improper administration of the dowries is convincing proof that the law does not include each local ordinary, but only him who is the local ordinary of the territory wherein the dowries are administered. In virtue of canon 2412, n. 1, he can inflict penalties, even to the deprivation of office, for spending the capital of the dowry. It would be contrary to fundamental legal principles to contend that a local ordinary could

---

[36] *Manuale Iuris Canonici,* p. 277, q. 208.
[37] *De Religiosis,* p. 506, n. 230.
[38] Cf. canon 550, § 2, and canon 512, § 2, n. 3.

inflict these penalties on a religious residing outside of his territory.[39]

Pruemmer seems to acknowledge the weakness of his opinion when he admits that because of the inconveniences involved in giving the account to each ordinary in whose diocese is found a house of the community, it is better to render the account only to the local ordinary of the diocese or archdiocese in which the dowries are actually administered.

The power given to local ordinaries in canon 535, § 1, n. 2, namely, to use appropriate remedies to correct the improper administration of the dotal funds if the accounting is unsatisfactory, extends only to monasteries of nuns. However, by reason of his jurisdiction over diocesan institutes he possesses the right to take similar measures against them if he does not approve the account. In pontifical congregations his power is more restricted. If the accounting is unsatisfactory he may proceed according to the general norms given for the canonical visitor. He may issue precepts and decrees which are binding on the community. A recourse against these precepts and decrees may of course be interposed with the Holy See. But such a recourse does not entail any suspensive effect regarding the ordinary's intervention, for in the language of the Code the recourse can be undertaken *"in devolutivo tantum,"* which implies that the canonical visitor's authoritative orders must be followed unless and until the Holy See makes a contrary provision for the case.[40]

If, however, the administrators of the dowries in a pontifical congregation, as well as in any other type or religious institute, are guilty of spending the capital sum in violation of the prohibition contained in canon 549, the local ordinary has the right and the duty to punish them in proportion to the gravity of their guilt, not excluding removal from office if the case demands it.[41]

---

[39] Cf. Reilly, *The Visitation of Religious,* The Catholic University of America, Canon Law Studies, No. 112 (Washington, D. C.: The Catholic University of America, 1938), pp. 92-93.

[40] Cf. canon 345.

[41] Cf. canon 2412, n. 1.

CHAPTER X

RESTITUTION OF THE DOWRY

The religious life is intended to be a permanent state for those who freely choose to leave the world and practice the Evangelical counsels in a religious community. Normally, those who enter religion do so with the hope and the intention of persevering in that vocation until death. No woman is admitted to religious profession until she has undergone at least a year of probation in the novitiate, during which time the candidate, on the one hand, has an opportunity of thoroughly acquainting herself with the religious life and its obligations, while the superioresses, on the other, have an opportunity of observing her and of judging whether or not she has a true vocation.

The normal permanent status of the religious life, however, is not so rigid as to exclude all exceptions in individual cases. Provision is made in the law of the Church permitting one who has entered religion to return to the world or to transfer to another community. For example, one who has made only temporary profession may, at the expiration of the term, be unwilling to renew her profession and choose to return to the lay state. Canon 637 permits her to do so. Or, a professed religious may make a petition for a dispensation from her vows, be they temporary or perpetual.[1] The present chapter deals with the disposal of the dowry in the event that the candidate who brought it departs, either by forsaking the religious life entirely, or by transferring to another community. The legislation of the Church on this point is contained in canon 551.

ARTICLE I. DEPARTURE OR DISMISSAL OF A RELIGIOUS

Canon 551, § 1: Dos religiosae professae sive votorum solemnium sive votorum simplicium quavis

---

[1] Cf. canon 638.

107

de causa discedenti integra restituenda est sine fructibus iam maturis.

Canon 551, § 1, states that when a professed religious with either solemn or simple vows leaves the institute, then her dowry must be returned to her in its entirety, without the interest which has already matured. The present law obliging the restitution of the dowry has equal application to solemn and simple vow institutes. Prior to the Code article 95 of the *Normae* of 1901 prescribed the return of the dowry to a sister who departed or was dismissed from a religious congregation.[2] In monasteries of nuns the original practice was to permit the monastery to retain the dowry of a departing nun, but in the course of time the jurisprudence of the Sacred Congregation of Bishops and Regulars showed an increasing tendency in favor of the restoration of the dowry to those nuns who left, especially if the monastery was at fault.[3]

It will be noticed that the law speaks of "professed religious." This term includes all those who have made any kind of valid profession in a religious community, except that which is made by special privilege at the point of death.[4] The term excludes postulants and novices. Nevertheless, there can be no doubt about the obligation of the institute to refund the dowry paid by either a postulant or a novice who departs without making profession. For in such cases the institute has no claim whatsoever to the dowry. The money or securities which represent the dowries are merely on deposit with the institute throughout the time during which the ones for whom the dowries were offered continue as postulants or novices in the community. All rights of the institute to the dotal funds are conditioned on the

---

[2] Cf. *supra,* p. 43.

[3] Cf. Goyeneche, "Consultationes,"—*CpRM,* V (1924), 391-392; *supra,* pp. 36-37.

[4] For an explanation of the privileges and effects of religious profession made at the point of death before the completion of the novitiate, cf. decr. S. C. de Rel., 30 dec. 1922—*AAS,* XV (1923), 156; cf. also "Annotationes," —*Periodica,* XII (1923), 41-42.

future profession of the candidate.[5] The obligation of returning the dowry to a departing postulant or novice arises, not from canon 551, § 1, but from canon 570, § 2.[6] The latter canon prescribes that if the postulant or novice leaves without making profession, all those things which she brought and which are not consumed by use must be returned to her. In the law prior to the Code the Holy See repeatedly insisted on the return of the dowry to a candidate who for any reason departed without making profession.[7] If a candidate dies during the postulate or novitiate, her dowry must be given to her heirs or to those persons whom she may have designated.[8]

"Quavis de causa discedenti"—The dowry must be returned to a professed religious who leaves her institute, no matter what be the cause of her departure. Therefore, it makes no difference whether she leaves voluntarily or under compulsion, whether she departs lawfully either after the expiration of her temporary vows or after having obtained a dispensation, or whether she departs unlawfully.[9] The application of this law to most forms of egress from the religious life is quite clear, but in a few instances, especially in the case of apostasy from religion, the few authors who treat the question are not agreed in their interpretation of the obligation to return the dowry. There can be no doubt that the law applies in all forms of departure wherein the juridical bond between the religious and the institute is completely and perpetually severed, so that the former religious is no longer in any sense a

---

[5] Cf. Larraona, "Commentarium Codicis,"—*CpRM,* XXI (1940), 146; Fuchs, "Rückgabe der Mitgift an die ausscheidende Klosterfrau,"—*ThPrQs,* LXXXVIII (1935), 362.

[6] Oesterle, *Praelectiones Iuris Canonici,* I, 302

[7] Cf. *supra,* p. 35.

[8] Chelodi, *Ius de Personis,* p. 443, n. 267, c); Cappello, *Summa,* II, p. 204, n. 604; cf. also canon 569, § 3.

[9] Fanfani, *De Iure Religiosorum,* p. 191, n. 171; Vromant, *De Bonis Ecclesiae Temporalibus,* p. 270, n. 256; cf. also Chelodi, *op. cit.,* p. 442, n. 267; Cappello, *loc. cit.;* Coronata, *Institutiones,* I, p. 727, n. 577, 5o; Gerster, *Ius Religiosorum,* p. 88; Jone, "Herausgabe der Mitgift einer Ordensschwester,"—*ThPrQs,* LXXXII (1929), 133; Toso, *Commentaria,* lib. II, pars II, p. 111, n. 1.

member of the organization.   Such a separation takes place in the
following ways:

a) By voluntary departure after the term of temporary vows
has expired; or by the refusal of the institute to allow the religious
to renew temporary vows or to make profession of perpetual
vows.[10]

b) By secularization, which implies that the woman religious
is reduced to the lay state in virtue of an indult.[11]

c) By the dismissal of a professed religious with temporary
vows.[12]

d) By the dismissal of a professed religious with perpetual
vows.[13]
In this case, although the legal bond is broken by the act of
dismissal and the one dismissed ceases to be a member of the
community, she nevertheless remains bound by the obligation of
her vows unless the constitutions of the organization or an
Apostolic indult declare otherwise.[14]

e) By the dismissal of a religious in either temporary or perpetual profession when she is guilty of any of the following
crimes, which are punished by automatic expulsion from the
religious life: an act of public apostasy from the Catholic faith;
the act of absconding with a person of the other sex; the act of
attempting or contracting matrimony, or also of entering into
a bond of civil marriage.[15]

In all the above cases the dowry must be returned, because
the egress is complete and juridical as well as permanent and
factual.   The religious has departed in the fullest sense of the
word and ceases to be a member of the institute.   Therefore,
by reason of canon 551, § 1, she has the right not merely in
charity, but in justice, to recover her dowry.[16]

-----

[10] Canon 637.
[11] Canons 638, 640.
[12] Canons 647, 648.
[13] Canons 651-653.
[14] Canon 669.
[15] Canon 646.
[16] Cf. Fuchs, "Rückgabe der Mitgift an die ausscheidende Klosterfrau,"—
ThPrQs, LXXXVIII (1935), 362-363.

Next to be considered are those cases wherein a factual departure has taken place without the severence of the juridical bond which unites the religious with the institute. Such a separation is unlawful when a religious is guilty either of apostasy from her religious institute or of flight from her religious house. It is lawful when she has been properly authorized by the competent ecclesiastical authority to live temporarily outside of her religious community. In pontifical institutes an indult for this purpose can be granted only by the Holy See, while in diocesan institutes it can be granted also by the local ordinary.[17] A religious who has obtained this permission continues to be a member of the institute, and she remains bound by the vows and all the other obligations of her profession compatible with her state of temporary separation from the community.[18] Upon the expiration of the term of the indult she is bound to return to the community. Thus it is seen that although such a religious has actually left the community, the separation is only partial and temporary, and does not seem to suffice to constitute departure from the relgious life in the sense of that mentioned in canon 551, § 1. It follows therefore that in such circumstances the institute is not bound to return the dowry to the absent religious.[19] The institute may, however, contribute to her support by giving her the income from her dowry.[20]

A *fugitive* is one who leaves the religious house without the permission of her superioress, but has the intention of returning.[21] She remains a member of the community, is bound by the obligation of her rule and vows and must return without delay. Furthermore, the superioress must seek her with solicitude, and

---

[17] Canon 638.

[18] Canon 639.

[19] Blat, *Commentarium,* II, p. 320, n. 342; Larraona, "Commentarium Codicis,"—*CpRM,* XXI (1940), 147; Fuchs, "Rückgabe der Mitgift an die ausscheidende Klosterfrau,"—*ThPrQs,* LXXXVIII (1935), 364. Eichmann holds the contrary opinion—"Die dos der Klosterfrau,"—*Theologie und Glaube,* XXVI (1934), 163.

[20] Blat, *loc. cit.*

[21] Canon 644, § 3.

receive her if she returns animated by sincere repentance.[22]   This unlawful and illegal separation is by its very nature temporary, and does not effect, in itself, a dismissal from the community. As in the previous case, this temporary absence, even though it be illegal, does not suffice to constitute a departure from the institute in the sense of canon 551, § 1.[23]   And therefore the dowry is not to be restored to her.

An *apostate* from the religious life is one who, after being professed with perpetual vows, either simple or solemn, unlawfully leaves the religious house with the intention of not returning, or who, having left the house legitimately, does not return because she intends to withdraw herself from religious obedience.[24] The malicious intention of disowning religious obedience is legally presumed if within one month the religious has neither returned nor manifested to her superioress her intention of returning.[25] The unlawful departure of an apostate from the religious house is similar to that of a fugitive, except that in the case of the former it is intended to constitute a permanent separation and withdrawal from the religious life.   The principal reason given above for the contention that the community is not bound to return the dowry either to a religious who has obtained a leave of absence, or to a religious who is classed as a fugitive from her religious house, is based upon the temporary nature of the separation of these religious from the institute.   Now, if the same criterion be invoked, but with a view to its inverted application, then it seems that the dowry should be restored to an apostate religious, not only after a formal decree of dismissal has been issued against her, but even apart from such a decree, once it becomes certain that she in no manner is willing to return.

Although the voluntary egress of an apostate religious from the religious house does not sever the juridical bond nor relieve her from the obligations of her vows, nevertheless, practically considered, a true and permanent departure from the institute

---

[22] Canon 645, §§ 1-2.
[23] Cf. Larraona, *loc. cit.;* Blat, *loc. cit.*
[24] Canon 644, § 1.
[25] Canon, 644, § 2.

has taken place, especially after she becomes adamant in her resolve not to return despite all the solicitous efforts on the part of her superioress to induce her to come back. A more precise wording in the Code to cover such a case would indeed be desirable. Nevertheless, the present wording seems to justify the conclusion that the institute should return the dowry to an apostate religious when it becomes certain that she will not return. It is not apparent that the expression *"quavis de causa discedenti"* of canon 551, § 1, presupposes a juridical dissolution of the bond in addition to a factual departure when the latter is complete and permanent, as is the case when all hope of the return of an apostate religious is abandoned. On the contrary, such a departure seems to come fully within the meaning of the law. Somewhat more specific than the present law is article 95 of the *Normae* of 1901, which states that if a religious departs or is dismissed (*discedat vel dimittatur*) from the institute her dowry is to be restored.[26] The wording of this article seems to urge the obligation of returning the dowry not only when the religious was legally dismissed (*dimittatur*), but also when she abandoned the community (*discedat*), even though no formal dismissal took place.

Arguments in support of the obligation to return the dowry to an apostate religious can be gathered not only from the text of the law, but also, as Larraona points out,[27] from the purpose of the law. It seems unjust, he says, for the institute to retain the income from the dowry destined for the support of the religious when that support is not given. Since the payment of the interest to an apostate religious by the institute would be beset with many difficulties, Larraona favors the return of the capital sum itself by means of which the institute would thus be liberated from giving the income to the apostate. Since the dowry must be returned to a dismissed religious even though she remains bound by her vows, it seems that it should likewise be returned to an apostate religious who definitely refuses to

---

[26] Cf. *supra,* p. 43.
[27] "Commentarium Codicis,"—*CpRM,* XXI (1940), p. 147, footnote 783.

return.[28]   For, although a decree of dismissal may not yet have been issued against the apostate religious, she can be dismissed by the process outlined in canons 651-652.

Not many of the authors discuss the question of the return of the dowry to a religious who has apostatized from the religious life. A few who comment briefly on the clause *"quavis de causa discedenti"* of canon 551, § 1, seem to imply the obligation of returning the dowry to an apostate religious, as well as to any other religious who leaves the institute, when they state that the dowry must be returned whether the religious departs freely or under compulsion, lawfully or unlawfully.[29]   Toso concludes that since the law prescribing the return of the dowry does not distinguish between the different forms of departure, the religious who has apostatized from the religious life should be considered as included among those to whom the dowry is to be restored.[30]

Mothon asserts that the dowry should be returned to an apostate religious if she claims it. He bases his opinion, first, on the cogent fact that canon 551, § 1, does not distinguish between legitimate and illegitimate departure. His second reason, namely, that the religious retains the ownership of her dowry during her life in the community is less convincing, since the more tenable opinion seems to be that the institute is the owner, although not irrevocably so until after the death of the religious.[31]   Mothon states that if the apostate religious on the other hand does not formally claim her dowry, the institute may keep it until such time when she is relieved of her vows and becomes legitimately capable of administering her property.[32]   This author's distinction, based on whether or not the apostate religious claims the dowry, seems to be entirely arbitrary and without any foundation in the law.

The principal arguments of those who assert that the institute is not bound to return the dowry to an apostate are based on

---

[28] Larraona, *loc. cit.*
[29] Cf. *supra*, p. 109.
[30] *Commentaria*, lib. II, pars II, p. 111, n. 1.
[31] Cf. *infra*, pp. 127-133.
[32] *Institutiones canoniques*, I, pp. 808-809, footnote 13.

the fact that the juridical bond is not broken and that the superior-ess is bound to try to bring about her return. However, as shown above, it is not evident that the law requires a juridical dis-solution of the bond in addition to the permanent factual departure of the apostate religious. And, furthermore, after repeated efforts of the superioress to induce the apostate religious to return have proved entirely fruitless, it becomes apparent that further efforts on her part are useless.

In summing up the question of the obligation of the institute to return the dowry, perhaps one will offer the best solution by making the distinction which Larraona makes. This author states that the wording of the Code extends to all forms of departure which from their nature are not temporary and pro-visional but permanent, whether they be lawful or unlawful, ju-ridical or factual.[33] The application of this distinction seems entirely justifiable and would simplify the solution of particular cases. Nevertheless, in view of the division of opinion among the authors, it should probably be conceded that a doubt of law exists and therefore that the institute cannot be compelled to return the dowry to an apostate religious until she has been canonically dismissed. In practice, however, even the authors who favor the interpretation that there is no obligation until the juridical bond is dissolved say that it is advisable to refund the dowry to an apostate religious as soon as all hope of her return is abandoned, in order to avoid unfavorable publicity and to avoid any appearance of self-interest in the condemnation of her apostasy.[34]

"Dos integra restituenda est"—Canon 551, § 1, prescribes that the *entire* capital sum of the dowry be restored to a professed religious who departs from the community. It is evident that the term *entire dowry* does not include gifts voluntarily given to the

---

[33] "Commentarium Codicis,"—*CpRM*, XXI (1940), 147.

[34] Creusen-Garesché-Ellis, *Religious Men and Women in the Code*, p. 145, n. 187; Fuchs, "Rückgabe der Mitgift an die ausscheidende Kloster-frau,"—*ThPrQs*, LXXXVIII (1935), 363; Beste, *Introductio in Codicem*, p. 368.

institute by the candidate before her profession.[25] In ordinary circumstances, that is, when the dowry has been paid in cash and when, in the course of the investment and administration of the funds, the value of the capital sum has remained unchanged, the institute fully complies with the law by returning the same amount of money as was given by the candidate to constitute her dowry.[36] It may happen, however, that the actual value of the funds representing the dowry has changed during the period in which the institute administered them. The question then arises as to what constitutes the *entire* dowry in the sense of canon 551, § 1. Is it the amount of the original payment, or is it the amount which represents the present value of the principal? A definite answer cannot be given to this question without taking into account a number of factors that have a bearing on the case. In the first place, any particular laws or private agreements are binding so long as they do not conflict with the common law.[37] If the invested dowries decrease in value, or even totally perish, the general rules of imputability and restitution apply.[38] Therefore, the institute is held responsible for the diminution or loss of the dowry due to maladministration; not, however, if the diminution or loss is the result of causes not culpably imputable to the institute. If the entire dowry has perished without the fault of the institute, there is no obligation from canon 551, § 1, to give anything to the departing religious.[39] But in such case,

---

[35] Cf. Fanfani, *De Iure Religiosorum*, p. 192, n. 171, dubium III; Larraona, "Commentarium Codicis,"—*CpRM*, XXI (1940), 148.

[36] Cf. Pruemmer, *Manuale Iuris Canonici*, p. 277, Q. 208, 5.

[37] E.g., the constitutions may require a dowry of $100 and prescribe that this identical amount be returned in the event the religious leaves, irrespective of any increase or decrease in the value of the corresponding investment.

[38] Cf. Vermeersch-Creusen, *Epitome*, I, p. 499-500, n. 700; Oesterle, *Praelectiones Iuris Canonici*, I, 302; Fanfani, *De Iure Religiosorum*, p. 191, n. 171, A); Larraona, "Commentarium Codicis,"—*CpRM*, XXI (1940), 149; Creusen, "Restitution d'une dot,"—*Revue des Communautés Religieuses*, I (1925), 151-152; Schaefer, *De Religiosis*, p. 508, n. 231; cf. also canons 536 and 2421, n. 1.

[39] Cf. Vermeersch-Creusen, *Epitome*, I, p. 500, n. 700; Fanfani, *De Iure Religiosorum*, p. 191, n. 171; Vromant, *De Bonis Ecclesiae Temporalibus*, p. 270, n. 256.

the institute is obliged to give her a charitable subsidy if she cannot provide for herself out of her own goods.[40]

Generally taken, the institute may return to a departing religious the actual securities which represent the dowry or the monetary equivalent. For a more specific determination of the quantity to be restored, authors say that if the dowry was paid in securities which are still retained by the institute, then these same securities are to be returned, irrespective of any change in value.[41] If one adopts the opinion which holds that the religious retains the ownership of the dowry during her profession, the assertion that the change in value of the above mentioned securities should not be taken into consideration when they are returned can be explained on the moral principle *"res perit domino."* It seems permissible to invoke this same principle even if one adopts the opinion which attributes to the institute a conditional or resolutory ownership of the dowry during the profession of the religious. For according to this opinion the religious does not relinquish all claim to the ownership of the dowry, and if she departs she herself becomes the ultimate owner of it. Thus the increase or decrease in the value of the securities is borne by the ultimate owner, whether that be the religious or the institute.

On the other hand, if the dowry was paid in cash which was later invested as prescribed by canon 549, or if the dowry was paid in securities and then reinvested, a distinction must be made. If each individual dowry is placed in a corresponding investment, so that an identity is retained between each dowry and the particular securities which represent it, then upon the departure of a religious these securities or their cash equivalent must be returned, whether or not the value has changed.[42] But when

---

[40] Cf. canon 643, § 2; resp., S. C. de Rel., 2 martii 1924—*AAS*, XVI (1924), 165-166.

[41] Cf. Schaefer, *De Religiosis,* p. 507, n. 231; Fanfani, *De Iure Religiosorum,* p. 192, n. 171; Vromant, *De Bonis Ecclesiae Temporalibus,* p. 272, n. 256; Creusen, "Restitution d'une dot,"—*Revue des Communautés Religieuses,* I (1925), 151; Fuchs, "Rückgabe der Mitgift an die ausscheidende Klosterfrau,"—*ThPrQs,* LXXXVIII (1935), 366; Coronata, *Institutiones,* I, p. 727, n. 577.

[42] Cf. Creusen, *loc. cit.;* Jombart, "Les dots,"—*Revue des Communautés Religieuses,* III (1927), 56; Larraona, "Commentarium Codicis,"—*CpRM,* XXI (1940), 150.

all or several of the dowries have been invested cumulatively, what amount is the institute bound to return to a departing religious if the amount representing the current value of her proportionate share of the investment does not correspond to the amount she paid upon entrance? Coronata[43] maintains that the same amount as was paid should be restored, since no account need be taken of the increase or decrease that may have taken place in the value of the invested funds. Larraona says that regularly this should be, and is, done. Nevertheless, he favors another method which seems to be more in conformity with the law and justice.[44] According to this plan a departing religious should be given her proportionate share of the current value of the cumulative investment.[45] For example, suppose that $1,000, representing ten dowries of $100 each, is invested cumulatively, and at the time of the departure of one of the religious the capital sum has advanced in value to $1,100. She should be given $110, for this amount represents her entire dowry (*dos integra*). The additional $10 does not represent the earned income, for this is separate and accrues to the institute, but represents, rather, the increase in the value of the securities themselves, and therefore seems to be a part of the capital sum. Since the capital of the dowry is not irrevocably acquired by the institute until the death of the religious, and since the *entire* dowry must be returned to a departing member, the institute seems to lack any title which would justify the withholding of the increased amount.[46] On the other hand, if through no fault in administration the capital sum decreases in value, the institute is not obliged to bear the loss. In the above example, if the total value had decreased to $900, then the institute would be bound to give only $90 to the departing religious,[47] for this sum represents the present entire capital of her dowry.

---

[43] *Institutiones*, I, p. 727, n. 577.

[44] *Ibid.*, p. 151, nn. 5-6, and footnote 792.

[45] Cf. Jombart, *loc. cit.*; Cance, *Le code de droit canonique*, II, 69. This procedure, of course, prescinds from any particular law or private agreement whereby the institute is required to return the precise quantity of the dowry which was paid by the candidate on her entrance into the community.

[46] Cf. Larraona, *ibid.*, p. 150, footnote 792.

[47] Cf. Jombart, *loc. cit.*

If, however, the decrease was so great that the refunded dowry is insufficient for the safe and proper return of a religious to her home and for providing a temporary decent livelihood, the institute is bound by canon 643, § 2, to supply the necessary additional funds as a charitable subsidy.[48]

"Sine fructibus iam maturis"—The income produced by the investment of the capital of the dowry is destined for the support of the religious during her life in the community. In some solemn vow institutes in which the required dowry is quite large the income may be sufficient to defray the entire cost of the support of the nun, but in most institutes wherein the members lead an active life the prescribed dowry is much smaller, for example, $100, with the result that the annual income from it far from equals the expenses incurred for the support of the member. Nevertheless, irrespective of the amount of the dowry or the type of religious organization, the institute acquires free and absolute title of ownership to the income from the invested dowries. This income is juridically distinct from the capital and accrues irrevocably to the institute. Therefore, in case a religious departs she can lay no claim whatsoever to the interest which has matured up to the time of her departure.[49] If, as is normally the case, the interest is collected on only one or a few specified days during the year, it is to be prorated from the time of the last collection up to the moment the religious leaves. For example, if the securities bear interest which is payable only on January 1 of each year and the religious leaves on July 1, the interest for that year is to be divided equally between the institute and the departing member. This method of computing matured interest is commonly accepted by most of the authors.[50] Coronata, on

---

[48] Cf. resp., S. C. de Rel., 2 martii 1924—*AAS*, XVI (1924), 165-166.

[49] Cf. canon 551, § 1; Larraona, "Commentarium Codicis,"—*CpRM*, XXI (1940), 152.

[50] Wernz-Vidal, *De Religiosis*, p. 225, n. 270; Vermeersch-Creusen, *Epitome*, I, p. 499, n. 700; Fanfani, *De Iure, Religiosorum*, p. 191, n. 171, A); Vromant, *De Bonis Ecclesiae Temporalibus*, p. 270, n. 256; Cocchi, *Commentarium*, IV, p. 143, n. 67, f; Blat, *Commentarium*, II, p. 319, n. 341; Fuchs, "Rückgabe der Mitgift an die ausscheidende Klosterfrau,"—*ThPrQs*, LXXXVIII (1935), 367; Larraona, *loc. cit.*

the contrary, adopts a different method. He defines matured interest as that which has actually been received or which could have been received and still can be collected at any time.[51] According to this author the institute in the above example would acquire no interest for the current year, because during the entire year the payment of interest remained suspended, and no part of the interest became mature until the actual day when the payment fell due, which in this case was after the religious had departed.

Against Coronata, the former method should be followed. For in financial transactions involving the payment and transfer of such securities as notes, stocks and bonds, the commonly accepted practice is to compute and divide the interest or dividend according to the length of time the securities are held by each possessor. This method of computing the matured income of investments is more in conformity with the purpose of the dowry which is to provide an income destined for the support of the religious during the entire time she receives that support from the community.

That the Holy See is solicitous concerning the fulfillment of the law prescribing the return of the dowry is evident from question 34 of the quinquennial report to be submitted by pontifical institutes. This question reads: "Has the entire dowry, however constituted, been returned to those who, for whatever reason, have left the institute, as well as the equipment which they brought with them to the institute and in the state in which it was at the time of their departure?"[52] Question 35 of the same report shows further the solicitude of the Holy See for the material welfare of the departing religious: "Has the institute, in the case of those who, received without a dowry and incapable of providing for themselves from their own resources, have left the institute, furnished them out of charity, on the occasion of their departure, with the means necessary for returning home safely and becomingly and for maintaining themselves decently for some time?"[53]

---

[51] *Institutiones,* I, p. 727, n. 577.
[52] Cf. Bouscaren, *The Canon Law Digest,* I, 287.
[53] Cf. Bouscaren, *loc. cit.*

ARTICLE II.   TRANSFER OF A RELIGIOUS TO ANOTHER INSTITUTE

Canon 551, § 2: Si vero religiosa professa ad aliam religionem ex apostolico indulto transeat, durante novitiatu, fructus, salvo praescripto canonis 570, § 1; emissa vero nova professione, dos ipsa huic religioni debentur; si ad aliud eiusdem Ordinis monasterium, huic debetur ipsa dos a die transitus.

The norms regulating the transfer of a religious from one institute to another are contained in canons 632-636 of the Code. The first of these canons states that a religious cannot transfer to another religious organization, even a stricter one, or from one independent monastery to another without authorization from the Holy See. When a transfer is thus effected canon 551, § 2, provides for the disposition of the dowry. This canon states that if a professed religious, by indult of the Holy See, transfers to another religious organization, the income from her dowry during the new novitiate must be given to the new community, without prejudice to the prescription of canon 570, § 1; after profession the capital of the dowry is to be transferred; but if the transfer is from one monastery to another of the same order, the second monastery has the right to the dowry from the day of the transfer.

The rule regulating the delivery of the *capital* of the dowry to the second institute is clear and presents no difficulty of interpretation. When the transfer is from one institute to another, a new novitiate must be made in the second, during which time the juridical bond between the religious and the first institute remains unbroken. If the religious fails to make profession in the new organization she must return to the former unless meanwhile the term of her vows has expired.[54] Because of the legal status existing between the religious and the first institute during the period of her novitiate in the second, it is clear why the Code forbids the transfer of the capital of the dowry until all ties with the original community have been completely and perpetually severed by the new profession.

---

[54] Canon 633, §§ 1-2.

The transfer of a religious to another monastery of the same order is effected in a somewhat different manner. She makes neither a new novitiate nor a new profession.[55] The cessation of her juridical connection with the first monastery is accomplished by the transfer itself, which also creates immediately a new bond between the religious and the second monastery. In other words, the obligations and effects of her profession are immediately and automatically transferred with her. Therefore, canon 551, § 2, logically prescribes that the new monastery has the right to the dowry from the day of the transfer.

The Code is silent about the disposition of the dowry if a religious transfers from one province to another within the same institute. Such a transfer and its effects are governed by the particular constitutions; and if these are silent on the matter, it would seem more conformable to the Code and the nature of the case to transfer the dowry to the new province.[56] This procedure supposes, of course, that the dowries are administered in each province, and not by the general superioress.[57]

The determination of the right to the *income* from the invested dowry during the period of the new novitiate when a religious transfers to another institute is the source of two divergent opinions among the authors. The reason for the divergence arises from the interpretation of the clause, *"salvo praescripto canonis 570, § 1,"* as contained in canon 551, § 2. According to canon 570, § 1, no compensation may be claimed for the expenditures of keeping a postulant or novice, except what the constitutions perhaps demand for food and clothing, or what was agreed upon for these purposes by an express agreement between the community and the entrant when the latter began her service as a postulant or as a novice.

The first of the two opinions attempts to reconcile the above two canons as follows: The interest from the dowry during the new novitiate must *always* be paid to the second institute. In addition, this institute has the right to demand compensation for

---

[55] Canon 633, § 3.
[56] Cf. Quaestio III—*Periodica*, X (1922), p. (12); Bastien, *Directoire canonique* (1923), p. 69, n. 105; Cappello, *Summa*, II, p. 205, n. 604.
[57] Cf. canon 550, § 1.

the support of the novice if such is permitted by the constitutions or if it has been expressly agreed upon before the beginning of the new novitiate.[58]

The other and more probable opinion gives this interpretation: The second institute has a right to the interest from the dowry during the period of the new novitiate *only* if the constitutions permit compensation to be demanded for food and clothing furnished to the novice, or if this was expressly agreed upon before the beginning of the new probation.[59]

The first opinion seems to misinterpret the force of the clause "without prejudice to the prescription of canon 570, § 1" (*salvo praescripto canonis 570, § 1*). This qualifying phrase indicates that the legislator desires the fulfillment of the law of canon 570, § 1, if it should come into conflict with canon 551, § 2. Now, if the interest from the dowry were given to the second institute when the constitutions did not permit anything to be exacted for the expenses of the novitiate, or when no express agreement had been entered into for such expenses, the prescription of canon 570, § 1, would be violated, and yet this is precisely what the restricting clause in canon 551, § 2, is designed to prevent.

If some such expression as "notwithstanding the prescript of canon 570, § 1," had been used, then the first opinion would be correct; canon 551, § 2, would prevail in case of conflict, and the interest from the dowry during the new novitiate would always go to the second institute. However, this is not the case, and therefore the second opinion seems to be the correct interpretation. In other words, the interest accrued from the invested dowry

---

[58] Cf. Oesterle, *Praelectiones Iuris Canonici*, I, 303; Beste, *Introductio in Codicem*, p. 368.

[59] Cf. Goyeneche, "De Transitu ad Aliam Religionem,"—*CpRM*, II (1921), 122; Creusen-Garesché-Ellis, *Religious Men and Women in the Code*, p. 146, n. 188; Cappello, *Summa*, II, p. 205, n. 604; Wernz-Vidal, *De Religiosis*, p. 225, n. 270; Vermeersch-Creusen, *Epitome*, I, p. 499, n. 700; Schaefer, *De Religiosis*, p. 508, n. 231; Coronata, *Institutiones*, I, p. 728, n. 577, b); Raus, *Institutiones Canonicae*, p. 302, n. 186, 3); Cocchi, *Commentarium*, IV, p. 144, n. 67, f); Fanfani, *De Iure Religiosorum*, p. 191, n. 171, B); Vromant, *De Bonis Ecclesiae Temporalibus*, p. 271, n. 256; DeMeester, *Compendium*, II, 437; Toso, *Commentaria*, lib. II, pars II, p. 112, n. 3; Papi, *Religious in Church Law*, p. 100.

during the new novitiate must be given to the second institute *only* when its constitutions permit the exaction of payment for the sustenance and the religious habit furnished to the novice, or when an express agreement for such payment had been entered into before the beginning of the novitiate. Furthermore, this interpretation is more in conformity with the old law which was adverse to any payments during the novitiate except those which were necessary for food and clothing.[60] According to the first opinion, the new institute would always receive the interest from the dowry, and could also claim full compensation for the above necessities of the novice. This broad interpretation is opposed not only to the spirit of the old law, but also to the spirit of the Code in canon 570, § 1.

If the institute to which a religious transfers requires, either in the constitutions or by express agreement, an amount in excess of the interest on the dowry for novitiate expenses, the first institute is under no obligation to supply the difference, but rather, the religious herself is obliged to arrange for the additional payment.[61] On the other hand, if the interest exceeds the amount prescribed or agreed to, then only that quantity is to be delivered which suffices to meet these expenses. The remainder is to be left with the first institute.[62]

The institute from which the religious transferred acquires full right of ownership over the interest accrued on the dowry during the new novitiate in those cases wherein the second institute has no right to that income.[63]

Normally, it would seem more equitable for the interest to be ceded to that community upon whom the burden of support rests,

[60] Cf. Goyeneche, *loc. cit.;* Concilium Tridentinum—Sessio XXV, *de regularibus et monialibus,* c. 16; Bouix, *Tractatus de Jure Regularium,* tom. I, pars IV, sect. III, c. III, q. II; Pellizzarius, *De Monialibus,* c. III, sect. II, n. 51; cf. also *supra,* p. 17.

[61] Goyeneche, *ibid.,* p. 123; Creusen-Garesché-Ellis, *loc. cit.;* Vromant, *loc. cit.*

[62] Cf. canons 570, § 1, and 635, n. 2; cf. also Goyeneche, *loc. cit.;* Blat, *op. cit.,* p. 321, n. 343.

[63] Cf. Vermeersch-Creusen, *loc. cit.;* Creusen-Garesché-Ellis, *loc. cit.;* Coronata, *loc. cit.;* Cappello, *loc. cit.;* Cocchi, *loc. cit.;* De Meester, *loc. cit.;* Vromant, *loc. cit.*

because the primary purpose of the interest from the invested dowry is to help supply the necessities of life for the religious. The delivery of such income to the new community can easily be made obligatory, in virtue of canon 551, § 2, and canon 570, § 1, by a pact between that community and the transferring religious for the payment of her food and clothing during the novitiate.

There seems to be no basis in the law to admit with Fanfani,[64] whose opinion Schaefer follows,[65] that the interest should be added to the capital and then share the same destination as the capital.[66]

If, in accordance with the above norms, the second community has a right to the interest during the new novitiate, and if the religious fails to complete that novitiate and returns to her original community,[67] the interest should be prorated and divided between the two institutes in proportion to the time she spent in each.[68]

ARTICLE III. ACQUISITION OF IRREVOCABLE TITLE

Canon 548: Dos monasterio seu religioni irrevocabiliter acquiritur per obitum religiosae, licet haec nonnisi vota temporaria nuncupaverit.

Canon 548 contains the norm for determining the final and irrevocable acquisition of the funds representing the capital of the dowry. As was seen above, the capital and the accrued interest constitute two distinct juridical entitites.[69] The interest, as it matures, is acquired unconditionally by the institute,[70] while the final destination of the capital remains in a state of uncertainty, depending on the perseverance of the religious who brought it. It for any reason she leaves the community, then the dowry, less

---

[64] *Loc. cit.*
[65] *Loc. cit.*
[66] Cf. Creusen-Garesché-Ellis, *op. cit.*, p. 147, n. 188.
[67] Cf. canon 633, § 2.
[68] Goyeneche, *ibid.*, p. 123.
[69] *Supra,* p. 119.
[70] Cf. canon 551, § 1.

the matured interest, is refunded to her,[71] but if she remains until death, then the institute acquires absolute and irrevocable title to it, even though she had taken temporary vows only.[72] The purposes for which the capital remains in a state similar to sequestration during the lifetime of the religious end with her death. The institute is freed from the obligation of supporting her, and there is no longer any need of keeping the capital available for restitution in case of departure. Thus all reasons for the former restrictions on the disposal of the funds are removed, and the dowry becomes incorporated into the treasury of the institute. In those organizations which have a centralized government the particular constitutions or custom may determine more definitely whether the dowry thus acquired goes to the entire institute, to the provinces, or to the local houses.[73]

Canon 548 is universal in its application, that is, it applies equally to all organizations of women religious without regard to the type of vows pronounced by the members. In every institute, even in those with perpetual profession, the first vows taken by all candidates for the religious life are only temporary—usually three years.[74] If a member dies at any time after that first temporary profession the institute automatically acquires irrevocable title to the dowry.[75] On the other hand, if a candidate dies while she is a postulant or a novice, even if she was admitted to profession at the point of death, her dowry, if it be on deposit with the institute, must be given to her heirs or to those whom she may have designated in her last will.[76]

The failure of the Code to designate the subject of the owner-

---

[71] Cf. canon 551, § 1.

[72] Cf. canon 548.

[73] Vermeersch-Creusen, *Epitome,* I, p. 500, n. 701; Wernz-Vidal, *De Religiosis,* p. 226, n. 271.

[74] Cf. canon 574, § 1; decr. *"Perpensis,"* S. C. Ep. et Reg., 3 martii 1902—*Fontes,* n. 2039.

[75] S. C. Ep. et Reg., *Ordinis Carmelitarum Excalceatorum,* 26 mart. 1904—*Fontes,* n. 2046.

[76] Cf. canons 548 and 569, § 1; Cappello, *Summa,* II, p. 204, n. 604; Chelodi, *Ius de Personis,* p. 443, n. 267; Schaefer, *De Religiosis,* p. 510, n. 232; Larraona, "Commentarium Codicis,"—*CpRM,* XX (1939), 306; decr. S. C. de Rel., 30 dec. 1922—*AAS,* XV (1923), 156-158.

ship of the dowry during the lifetime of the religious has given rise to different opinions among the authors. This omission in the law and the divergence of opinion of the authors make it impossible for one to solve the question with satisfactory finality. Nevertheless an explanation of the two opinions as well as a consideration of the arguments advanced in support of each will help one to form a judgment in the matter even though a definite and conclusive solution cannot be reached.

Briefly, the two opinions advanced are as follows. The first asserts that a conditional resolutory ownership of the dowry passes to the institute at the time of the first profession of the candidate. Then at the death of the religious who perseveres in the institute, that ownership automatically becomes absolute and irrevocable.[77] The other opinion asserts that the religious herself retains ownership of the dowry until her death. During her life in the community the institute has full power of administration as well as the exclusive right to the interest earned from the investment of the dowry, but the institute does not acquire any form of ownership of it until the death of the religious, at which time absolute ownership passes automatically to the institute.[78]

In the first place it must be clearly understood that the same method of acquisition of the dowry pertains equally to institutes whose members have solemn vows and to institutes whose members have only simple vows. Canon 548 states expressly that the dowry is acquired irrevocably by the monastery *or* the institute at the death of the religious, even though she has taken only

---

[77] Cf. Larraona, "De Dote Religiosarum in Codice Iuris Canonici,"— *CpRM,* XIX (1938), 19-30; D'Ambrosio, "De Radicali Dominio Dotis Religiosarum,"—*Apollinaris,* I (1928), 173-176; Blat, *Commentarium,* II, p. 314, n. 332; Vermeersch-Creusen, *Epitome,* I, p. 500, n. 701; Schaefer, *De Religiosis,* pp. 509-510, n. 232; Wernz-Vidal, *De Religiosis,* pp. 226-227, n. 271; Coronata, *Institutiones,* I, p. 726, n. 577; Haring, *Grundzüge des katholischen Kirchenrechtes,* II, p. 782, footnote 6; Beste, *Introductio in Codicem,* p. 367; De Meester, *Compendium,* II, p. 437, footnote 5.

[78] Cf. Eichmann, "Die dos der Klosterfrau,"—*Theologie und Glaube,* XXVI (1934), 161-176; Leitner, *Das Ordensrecht,* p. 392; Mayer, *Benediktinisches Ordensrecht in der Beuroner Kongregation,* III, 71-76; Bastien, *Directoire canonique* (1923), p. 67, n. 102; Fuchs, "Rückgabe der Mitgift an die ausscheidende Klosterfrau,"—*ThPrQs,* LXXXVIII (1935), 362.

temporary vows. Some of the difficulties inherent in one or the other of the two above opinions do not involve both types of religious institutes. However, it must be borne in mind that the correct solution, whatever it may be, must be applicable to monasteries as well as to religious congregations.

This much is certain, namely, that the unification of the dotal law of the Code introduced a change in the former discipline. Prior to the Code, women religious in simple vows retained during their lifetime the ownership of their dowry, while the power of administration as well as the exclusive right to the accrued income pertained to the institute. If such a religious departed she recovered the capital of her dowry, but if she continued in her membership until death the title of ownership passed to the institute.[79] Mayer states that the Code not only retains these norms regarding the ownership and restitution of the dowry for religious who are professed with simple vows, but extends and applies the same regulations to all types of institutes of women religious without distinction as to whether the members take simple or solemn, temporary or perpetual vows.[80]

Larraona does not accept this explanation for the unification of the law on dowry in the Code. He grants that in regard to *restitution* the present uniform rule came about by adopting the former law which existed for religious professed with simple vows. However, this author denies that in regard to the *ownership* of the dowry the Code adopted for all institutes the former law existing for those societies whose members took only simple vows. His strongest argument is taken from the nature of the solemn vow of poverty. He states that since it is not evident that the Code wishes to derogate from the solemn vow of poverty by making an exception for the religious to retain the ownership of her dowry, the old law—in accordance with the norm of canon 6, n. 4—must be retained.[81]

The solemn vow of poverty presents the most formidable

---

[79] Cf. *Normae* of 1901, art. 95; decr. *Perpensis*, n. 13, S. C. Ep. et Reg., 3 maii 1902—*Fontes*, n. 2039.

[80] *Benediktinisches Ordensrecht in der Beuroner Kongregation*, III, 75.

[81] "De Dote Religiosarum in Codice Iuris Canonici,"—*CpRM*, XIX (1938), 23, footnote 6.

obstacle to the acceptance of the opinion which attributes the radical ownership of the dowry during the time of her profession to the religious herself. No one will deny that it is entirely within the power of the supreme legislator in the Church to modify the absolute and perfect renunciation of property which in the past has been associated with the solemn vow of poverty. Whether in fact the legislator has done so with regard to the dowry of women religious remains a disputed point. The text of canon 581, § 1, considered in itself, leads one to the conclusion that the renunciation of the solemnly professed religious is perfect and all embracing.[82] Nevertheless it is asserted that the right inherent in the claim which a religious has to the restitution of her dowry demands that notwithstanding her solemn vow of poverty she be allowed radically to retain ownership of the dowry against the day when she can in justice claim it as her own. In other words, the total renunciation of property at the time of solemn profession is modified and relaxed to the extent that a religious is allowed to retain the ownership, although not the possession and administration, of her dowry.[83] In this regard the significant point about canon 581, § 1, is the omission therein of any mention of an exception to the absolute and universal application of the renunciation of property by the religious. In view of the fact that by the solemn vow of poverty a religious voluntarily surrenders one of her fundamental rights, it does not seem unreasonable to assume that if the supreme legislator had intended any exceptions to be made with reference to that renunciation he would have made express mention of it. This is particularly true because of the traditional conception and juridical effect of the solemn vow of poverty. Larraona states that not even a remote basis can be found in the Code in support of the contention that a religious in solemn vows is by way of exception permitted

---

[82] Professus a votis simplicibus antea nequit valide, sed intra sexaginta dies ante professionem sollemnem, salvis peculiaribus indultis a Sancta Sede concessis, debet *omnibus bonis* quae actu habet, cui maluerit, sub conditione secuturae professionis, renuntiare.

[83] Cf. Mayer, *loc. cit.;* Eichmann, "Die dos der Klosterfrau,"—*Theologie und Glaube,* XXVI (1934), 174.

to retain the ownership of her dowry.[84] No matter which opinion one takes with respect to the passing of ownership of the dowry to the institute, a legal difficulty arises in the event that a religious in solemn vows is dismissed from the monastery. Canon 669 states that such a one remains bound by her vows (unless the constitutions of the organization or Apostolic indults declare otherwise), and therefore she is incapable of either owning or administering property. And yet, by virtue of canon 551, § 1, the monastery is bound to return the dowry to her. In order to reconcile these two canons and to avoid the juridical inconsistency which would follow if both retained their full force, it seems that it must be granted that the vow of poverty is relaxed in this case at least to an extent that will permit the institute to return the dowry.

According to the opinion which attributes ownership to the institute, the claim which the religious has to the restitution of her dowry is explained by a resolutory condition attached to the revocable transfer of ownership at the first profession. The dowry is destined for the support of the religious during the time in which she lives in the institute. If she leaves, the resolutory condition is fulfilled and its nullifying effect becomes operative, with the result that the ownership of the dowry automatically reverts to the person of the religious.[85] According to this explanation of the acquisition of the dowry the rights of both the religious and the institute are protected and there is no necessity to derogate from the universality of the renunciation of property which the religious makes at her solemn profession.

In support of the same opinion as that defended in the previous paragraph some authors attach a seemingly unwarranted significance to the meaning of the word *"irrevocabiliter"* in canon 548.[86] From the fact that this canon states that the dowry is acquired irrevocably at the death of the religious, these authors conclude that

---

[84] *Ibid.,* p. 22.

[85] Cf. D'Ambrosio, "De Radicali Dominio Dotis Religiosarum,"—*Apollinaris,* I (1928), 173; Larraona, "De Dote Religiosarum in Codice Iuris Canonici,"—*CpRM,* XIX (1938), 23, footnote 6.

[86] Dos monasterio seu religioni irrevocabiliter acquiritur per obitum religiosae, licet haec nonnisi vota temporaria nuncupaverit.

a previous revocable acquisition is implied. While this interpretation remains possible in view of the wording of the text, its argumentative force is inconclusive, for an irrevocable ownership could be acquired even without a previous revocable ownership. Eichmann minimizes the force of the argument which D'Ambrosio draws from the word *"irrevocabiliter."* He prefers to consider this word as emphasizing the force of the verb *"acquiritur"* which it modifies, and he says that its use is occasioned by the uncertainty of the ultimate fate of the dowry. Before the death of the religious it is uncertain into whose hands the dowry will eventually fall. With her death the status of the dowry is definitely and irrevocably determined.[87]

Another argument of doubtful probative value which is given in support of the view that the institute acquires a revocable ownership of the dowry at the first profession of the religious is taken from canon 547, § 2, where it is stated that the dowry shall be handed over (*tradatur*) to the monastery before the reception of the habit, or at least that its delivery be assured in a legal form recognized by the civil law. Larraona maintains that since this delivery or promise of delivery is in no way limited in the Code to a transfer of mere possession, it ought to be understood as effecting a transfer of ownership. To restrict the delivery to a transfer of possession only, he says, is to place an arbitrary restriction on the effect of that delivery.[88] Eichmann, however, argues that from the wording of canon 547, § 2, it is more probable that possession and not ownership is involved in the delivery of the dowry, for otherwise, he says, a more definite terminology such as that used in canons 582, n. 2, and 1299, § 1, would be employed.[89]

Vermeersch-Creusen question the right of the superioress to invest the dowry unless it be admitted that the institute acquires ownership of the dotal funds at the profession of the religious.[90] The evident answer to this objection is the fact that an ad-

---

[87] Eichmann, "Die dos der Klosterfrau,"—*Theologie und Glaube*, XXVI (1934), 175.

[88] *Ibid.*, p. 22.

[89] These canons speak of the acquisition of property *in proprietatem*.

[90] *Epitome*, I, p. 500, n. 701.

ministrator or trustee has the right to invest the money entrusted
to his care.[91]   These same authors question the right of the
institute to acquire the dowry at the death of a religious who is
professed with temporary vows, unless it be granted that the
institute has already become the owner of the dowry. This contention is likewise easily refuted. The Code definitely states that
the dowry is acquired irrevocably by the institute at the death of
the religious, even though she had taken only temporary vows. A
candidate who pays a dowry and enters the religious life tacitly
agrees to the legislation of the Church regulating the administration and acquisition of the dowry, and her heirs have no claim
against the clear provisions of the law.[92]

Eichmann uses an argument taken from canon 635, n. 2, to
support his contention that the religious retains the ownership of
her dowry. This canon determines certain property rights in the
event that a religious transfers from one monastery or congregation to another. It states that the former institute retains those
goods over which it has acquired ownership by reason of the
religious, but that this same institute must transfer to the new
community the capital of the dowry (in accordance with the norm
of canon 551, § 2) and the other personal goods of the religious.
Eichmann concludes from the prescriptions of this canon that
the dowry is not among the property over which the institute
obtains an acquired right during the lifetime of the religious, but
rather, that it is to be classed with the personal goods of the
religious even after solemn profession. He adds that since the
Code does not distinguish between revocable and irrevocable
ownership, it is not permitted that such a distinction be made.[93]
Larraona answers this argument by insisting that canon 548
justifies the assertion that the Code contemplates a revocable as
well as an irrevocable ownership of the dowry. He states that
canon 635, n. 2, classifies the dowry as personal property of the
religious only insofar as the acquired right of the institute is not
definitive during the lifetime of the religious.[94]

---

[91] Cf. Eichmann, *ibid.,* p. 173.

[92] Cf. Eichmann, *loc. cit.*

[93] *Ibid.,* pp. 174-175.

[94] "De Dote Religiosarum in Codice Iuris Canonici,"—*CpRM*, XIX (1938),
26.

When one endeavors to form a judgment in deciding which view to accept with reference to the manner of acquisition of ownership of the dowry he is faced with the necessity of basing his opinion upon arguments that are not entirely conclusive. Authors who treat the question give reasons in support of one or the other opinion, but they admit that the uncertainty of the law makes either opinion juridically possible. From the standpoint of practical advantages, each opinion has points in its favor. For example, in the event of secularization of religious institutes by the state the dowry could perhaps be spared if it pertained to the personal property of the individual religious.[95] On the other hand, if the ownership passes to the institute at the profession of the religious all the civil formalities of testamentary succession and the possibilities of trouble and expenses inherent therein are avoided.[96] However, these and other similar advantages in favor of one or the other opinion are, after the fact, of little help in deciding the intention of the legislator at the time of the formulation of the law. Without denying the probability of the other view, the writer considers more tenable the opinion which attributes the ownership of the dowry to the institute. The principal reason for adopting this view is that it offers a more satisfactory solution of the difficulty involved in regard to the juridical effects of the solemn vow of poverty.

A problem involving the irrevocable acquisition of the dowry may arise if a nun who made solemn profession before the promulgation of the Code leaves the monastery or transfers to another institute after the law of the Code went into effect. The question is whether or not canon 551, which prescribes the restitution of the dowry, applies in this case. Some authors answer in the affirmative,[97] but the negative seems rather to supply the correct answer because of the right acquired by the monastery at the solemn profession of the nun.[98] For under the former discipline

---

[95] Cf. Eichmann, *ibid.*, p. 174.

[96] Cf. Larraona, *ibid.*, p. 27.

[97] Fuchs, Rückgabe der Mitgift an die ausscheidende Klosterfrau,"— *ThPrQs*, LXXXVIII (1935), 364-365; Goyeneche, "Consultationes,"— *CpRM*, V (1924), 392; Coronata, *Institutiones*, I, p. 728, n. 577.

[98] Cf. Vermeersch-Creusen, *Epitome*, I, p. 500, n. 702; D'Ambrosio, "De

one of the legal effects of solemn profession was the transfer of irrevocable dominion of the dowry to the monastery.[99] In virtue of canon 4 that right of the monastery is protected against the obligation of restitution contained in the present law. According to canon 4 acquired rights acknowledged by the Holy See before the Code remain in force, unless they are explicitly revoked by the canons of the Code.

Since canon 551 makes no distinction as to the time when the vows were taken, Goyeneche concludes that the law of restitution applies in the case under consideration. In order that a law be binding, he says, it is requisite, but it also suffices, that the conditions which are incorporated in the law be actually present, as they are in this case.[100] However, he fails to take into account the protection given to acquired rights by canon 4.

The best solution seems to be that the case should be decided according to the norm existing under the old law. If before the Code the necessity of the transfer of a nun was occasioned by the monastery, the Holy See demanded the restitution of the dowry, but if she transferred voluntarily without any fault of the monastery there was no obligation of restitution, although in this latter case the Holy See usually requested that the institute assist the religious to raise a new dowry if she could not do so herself. It seems necessary to evaluate the acquired rights of the monastery in accordance with these norms of the former law, for although canon 4 protects those rights it does not increase or extend them beyond their original limits.

This problem does not arise in the case of sisters with simple vows, because for them the former law concerning the restitution of the dowry was the same as that of the Code.[101]

Dote Monialis ante Codicis Promulgationem Solemniter Professae et ad aliud Monasterium post Codicem Transeuntis,"—*Apollinaris,* I (1928), 297-300; Wernz-Vidal, *De Religiosis,* p. 226, footnote 21.

[99] Cf. *supra,* p. 36.

[100] Cf. *loc. cit.*

[101] Cf. art. 95, *Normae* of 1901; art. 13, decr. S. C. Ep. et Reg., *"Perpensis,"* 3 maii 1902—*Fontes,* n. 2039; canon 551.

CONCLUSIONS

From the foregoing study the following conclusions have been reached:

1. That legislation on the dowry of women religious was not introduced until after the Council of Trent.

2. That the payment of a dowry should in no way be confused with the crime of simoniacal purchase of entrance into the religious life.

3. That in congregations of simple vows wherein the religious engage in charitable or educational enterprises, from which they derive an income which in whole or in part covers the cost of their material sustenance, there is less need for a dowry, and the amount required is smaller than that which is demanded by contemplative orders.

4. That in addition to cash, securities which conform to the requirements of canon 549 may be accepted as payment of the dowry.

5. That special qualifications such as a teacher's certificate or a nurse's degree are not to be considered as the equivalent of a dowry, but may often constitute a sufficient cause for seeking a dispensation from the payment of the stipulated sum.

6. That in the administration of dowries the term "local ordinary" refers only to the ordinary of the territory wherein the dotal funds are actually administered.

7. That the permanent factual departure of an apostate religious seems to be a sufficient juridical cause to oblige the institute to refund her dowry.

8. That the opinion seems more tenable which attributes the ownership of the dowry, during the lifetime of the professed religious, to the institute rather than to the religious herself.

9. That the congregation to which a religious transfers is entitled to the income from the invested dowry during the new novitiate only when the constitutions of this institute permit compensation to be demanded for the food and clothing furnished to the novice, or when payment for these purposes was expressly agreed upon before the beginning of the novitiate.

BIBLIOGRAPHY

SOURCES

Acta Apostolicae Sedis, Commentarium Officiale, Romae, 1909—

Acta Ecclesiae Mediolanensis ab eius Initiis usque ad Nostram Aetatem, edited by Achille Ratti, 3 vols., Mediolani, 1890-1892.

Bullarii Diplomatum et Privilegiorum Sanctorum Romanorum Pontificum Taurinensis Editio, 24 vols., 1857-1872.

Canones et Decreta Sacrosancti Oecumenici Concilii Tridentini, Romae, 1904.

Codex Iuris Canonici Pii X Pontificis Maximi Iussu Digestus Benedicti Papae XV Auctoritate Promulgatus, Romae: Typis Polyglottis Vaticanis, 1917.

Codicis Iuris Canonici Fontes cura Emi. Petri Card. Gasparri Editi, 9 vols., Romae (later Civitate Vaticana): Typis Polyglottis Vaticanis, 1923-1939. (Vols. VII-IX *ed. cura et studio Emi. Iustiniani Card. Serédi.*)

Collectanea in Usum Secretariae Sacrae Congregationis Episcoporum et Regularium, 2. ed., Bizzarri, Romae, 1885.

Corpus Iuris Canonici, editio Lipsiensis II (Richter-Friedberg), 2 vols., Lipsiae, 1922.

Corpus Iuris Civilis (Krueger-Mommsen-Schoell-Kroll), Berolini: Apud Weidmannos, 1928-1929.

Decretales D. Gregorii Papae IX, una cum Glossa Restitutae, Romae, 1582.

Harduin, Jean, *Acta Conciliorum et Epistolae Decretales ac Constitutiones Summorum Pontificum,* 12 vols., Parisiis, 1715.

Hefele, Carolus, et Leclercq, Henricus, *Histoire des Conciles,* 10 vols. in 19, Paris, 1907-1938.

Mansi, Joannes, *Sacrorum Conciliorum Nova et Amplissima Collectio,* 53 vols., Parisiis, 1901-1927.

Normae Secundum quas S. Cong. Episcoporum et Regularium Procedere Solet in Approbandis Novis Institutis Votorum Simplicium, Romae: Typis S. Cong. de Propaganda Fide, 1901.

Pallottini, S., *Collectio Omnium Conciliorum et Resolutionum Quae in Causis Propositis Apud Sacram Congregationem Cardinalium S. Concilii Tridentini Interpretum Prodierunt ab eius Institutione anno MDLXIV ad annum MDCCCLX, Distinctis Titulis Alphabetico Ordine per Materias Digesta,* 17 vols., Romae, 1868-1893.

Thesaurus Resolutionum Sacrae Congregationis Concilii, 167 vols., Romae, 1718-1908.

AUTHORS

Allies, Thomas W., *The Monastic Life,* London, 1896.

Bachofen, Charles Augustine, *Compendium Juris Regularium,* New York, 1903.

——, *A Commentary on the New Code of Canon Law,* 8 vols., Vol. III (*Religious and Laymen*), 5. ed., St. Louis: Herder, 1938.

Balmes, Hilaire, *Les religieux à voeux simples d'après le code,* Paray-le-Monial, 1921.

Barbosa, Augustinus, *Iuris Ecclesiastici Universi Libri III,* Lugduni, 1660.

Bastien, Pierre, *Directoire canonique a l'usage des Congrégations à voeux simples,* Maredsous, 1904. Also, 3. ed., Bruges, 1923.

Battandier, Albert, *Guide canonique pour les constitutions des instituts à voeux simples,* Rome, 1898. Also, 6. ed., Paris, 1923.

Benedict XIV, *De Synodo Dioecesana,* 3 vols., Romae, 1788.

Beste, Udalricus, *Introductio in Codicem,* Collegeville: St. John's Abbey Press, 1938.

Blat, Alberto, *Commentarium Textus Codicis Iuris Canonici,* 6 vols., Vol. II (*Ius de Religiosis et Laicis Iuxta Codicis Ordinem*), 3. ed., Romae: Apud Angelicum, 1938.

Bonaventura, S., *Opera Omnia,* Quaracchi edition, 10 vols., 1882-1902.

Bouix, D., *Tractatus de Jure Regularium,* 2 vols., Parisiis, 1882.

Bouscaren, T. Lincoln, *The Canon Law Digest,* 3 vols., Milwaukee: Bruce, 1934-1938.

Brunini, Joseph Bernard, *The Clerical Obligations of Canons 139 and 142,* The Catholic University of America, Canon Law Studies, No. 103, Washington, D. C.: The Catholic University of America, 1937.

Cance, Adrien, *Le Code de droit canonique,* 3 vols., Vol. II, Paris: Gabalda et Fils, 1928.

Cabassutius, Joannes, *Iuris Canonici Theoria et Praxis,* Lugduni, 1678.

Cappello, Felix M., *Summa Iuris Canonici in Usum Scholarum Concinnata,* 3 vols., Vol. II, 3. ed., Romae: Apud Aedes Universitatis Gregorianae, 1939.

Cajetanus, Felix, *Juris Canonici Universi Commentarius,* 3 vols., Monachii, 1705.

Catholic Encyclopedia, 15 vols., New York, 1907-1912.

Chelodi, Ioannis, *Ius de Personis iuxta Codicem Iuris Canonici,* 2. ed., Tridenti: Libr. Editr. Tridentum, 1927.

Cocchi, Guidus, *Commentarium in Codicem Iuris Canonici ad Usum Scholarum,* 8 vols., Vol. IV, 3. ed., Taurinorum Augustae: Marietti, 1932.

Coronata, Matthaeus Conte a, *Institutiones Iuris Canonici,* 5 vols., Vol. I, 2. ed., Taurini (Italia): Marietti, 1939.

Creusen, J., *Religieux et Religieuses d'après le droit ecclesiastique,* 3. ed., Bruxelles: Dewit, 1924.

Creusen, Joseph-Garesché, Edward F.-Ellis, Adam C., *Religious Men and Women in the Code,* 3. English ed., Milwaukee: Bruce, 1940.

Currier, C. W., *History of Religious Orders,* New York, 1894.

De Luca, Joannes Baptista, *Theatrum Veritatis et Justitiae,* 16 vols. in 9, Coloniae Agrippinae, 1706.

138   *Dowry of Women Religious*

DeMeester, Alphonsus, *Juris Canonici et Juris Canonico-Civilis Compendium,* nova ed., 3 vols. in 4, Brugis, 1921-1928.

Eckenstein, Lina, *Woman Under Monasticism,* Cambridge, 1896.

Fanfani, Ludovicus, *De Iure Religiosorum ad Normam Codicis Iuris Canonici,* 2. ed., Taurini-Romae: Marietti, 1925.

Fagnanus, Prosperus, *Commentarium in Librum Decretalium,* 3 vols., Venetiis, 1709.

Ferraris, F. Lucius, *Prompta Bibliotheca, Canonica, Juridica, Moralis, Theologica, nec non Ascetica, Polemica, Rubricistica, Historica,* 9 vols., Rome, 1885-1899.

Ferreres, Ioannes B., *Institutiones Canonicae,* 2 vols., Barcinone: Eugenius Subirana, 1920.

Frey, Wolfgang, N., *The Act of Religious Profession,* The Catholic University of America, Canon Law Studies, No. 63, Washington, D. C.: The Catholic University of America, 1931.

Gerster, Thoma Villanova a Zeil, *Ius Religiosorum in Compendium Redactum,* Taurini: Marietti, 1935.

Geser, Fintan, *The Canon Law Governing Communities of Sisters,* St. Louis: Herder, 1938.

Gibalinus, Josephus, *Universa Tractatio Theologica et Canonica de Simonia,* Lugduni, 1659.

Gonzalez-Tellez, Emanuel, *Commentaria Perpetua in Singulos Textus quinque Librorum Decretalium Gregorii IX,* 5 vols. in 4, Venetiis, 1699.

Haring, Johann B., *Grundzüge des katholischen Kirchenrechtes,* 2 vols., Graz, 1924.

Jardi, Antonio de la C., *El Derecho de las Religiosas según las Prescripciones Vigentes del Codigo Canónico y Civil,* 2. ed., Vich: Serafica, 1927.

Kiekhofer, William H., *Economic Principles, Problems, and Policies,* New York: Appleton-Century, 1936.

Kober, F., *Die Suspension,* Tübingen, 1862.

Lanslots, D. I., *Handbook of Canon Law for Congregations of Women Under Simple Vows,* 6. ed., New York, 1911.

Leitner, Martin, *Handbuch des katholischen Kirchenrechts,* Dritte Leiferung: *Das Ordensrecht,* 2. ed., Regensburg: Kösel und Pustet, 1922.

Lucidi, Angelus, *De Visitatione Sacrorum Liminum Instructio S. C. Concilii,* 3 vols., Romae, 1883.

Mayer, Heinrich Suso, *Benediktinisches Ordensrechts in der Beuroner Kongregation,* 4 vols., Vol. III, Beuron, 1936.

McManus, James Edward, *The Administration of Temporal Goods in Religious Institutes,* The Catholic University of America, Canon Law Studies, No. 109, Washington, D. C.: The Catholic University of America, 1937.

Migne, Jacques Paul, *Patrologiae Cursus Completus, Series Graeca,* 161 vols., Parisiis, 1856-1866.

——, *Patrologiae Cursus Completus, Series Latina,* 221 vols., Parisiis, 1844-1864.

Mocchegiani, Petro, *Iurisprudentia Ecclesiastica ad Usum et Commoditatem utriusque Cleri*, 3 vols., Vol. I, Quaracchi ed., 1904.

Monacelli, Francesco, *Formularium Legale Practicum Fori Ecclesiastici*, 4 vols. in 3, Romae, 1884.

Montalembert, Count de, *The Monks of the West*, 2 vols., New York, 1860.

Mothon, Joseph Pie, *Institutions canoniques*, 3 vols., Paris: Desclée, 1922.

Oesterle, Gerardus, *Praelectiones Iuris Canonici*, Vol. I, Romae, 1931.

Ojetti, Benedetto, *Synopsis Rerum Moralium et Iuris Pontificii*, 3 vols., Vol. II, 3. ed., Romae, 1911.

Papi, Hector, *Religious in Church Law*, New York: Kenedy, 1924.

Pejska, Iosephus, *Ius Canonicum Religiosorum*, 3. ed., Friburgi Brisgoviae: Herder, 1927.

Pellizzarius, Franciscus, *Tractatio de Monialibus*, editio novissima, Romae, 1761.

Pennacchi, Josephus, *Commentaria in Constitutionem Apostolicae Sedis*, 2 vols., Romae, 1883.

Petra, Vincentius, *Commentaria ad Constitutiones Apostolicas*, 5 vols. in 2, Venetiis, 1729.

Piatus, Montensis, *Praelectiones Juris Regularis*, 3. ed., 2 vols., Tornaci, 1906.

Pignatelli, Jacobus, *Consultationes Canonicae*, 11 vols. in 4, Coloniae Allobrogum, 1700.

Pirhing, Ernricus, *Jus Canonicum Nova Methodo Explicatum*, 5 vols. in 4, Dilingae, 1674-1678.

Pruemmer, Dominicus M., *Manuale Iuris Canonici in Usum Scholarum*, 4. et 5. eds., Friburgi Brisgoviae: Herder, 1927.

Raus, P. J. B., *Institutiones Canonicae juxta Novum Codicem Juris*, 2. ed., Parisiis: Vitte, 1931.

Reiffenstuel, Anacletus, *Ius Canonicum Universum*, 5 vols. in 7, Parisiis, 1864-1870.

Reilly, Thomas Francis, *The Visitation of Religious*, The Catholic University of America, Canon Law Studies, No. 112, Washington, D. C.: The Catholic University of America, 1938.

Rodericus, Emanuel, *Quaestiones Regulares et Canonicae Enucleatae, sive Resolutiones Quaestionum Regularium*, Lugduni, 1634.

Santi-Leitner, *Praelectiones Juris Canonici*, 4. ed., 5 vols. in 3, Ratisbonae, 1903-1905.

Schaaf, Valentine Theodore, *The Cloister*, The Catholic University of America, Canon Law Studies, No. 13, Washington, D. C.: The Catholic University of America, 1921.

Schaefer, Timotheus, *Compendium de Religiosis ad normam Codicis Iuris Canonici*, 3. ed., Roma: S. A. L. E. R., 1940.

Schmalzgrueber, Franciscus, *Ius Ecclesiasticum Universum*, 5 vols. in 12, Romae, 1843-1845.

Schroeder, H. J., *Disciplinary Decrees of the General Councils*, St. Louis: Herder, 1937.

Suarez, Franciscus, *Opera Omnia,* 26 vols., Parisiis, 1856-1866.

Thomas, Aquinas, St., *Summa Theologica,* 6 vols., Taurini (Italia) : Marietti, 1936.

Thomassinus, Ludovicus, *Vetus et Nova Ecclesiae Disciplinae circa Beneficia et Beneficiarios,* 10 vols., Moguntiae, 1787.

Toso, Albertus, *Ad Codicem Iuris Canonici Commentaria Minora,* 5 vols., Lib. II, pars II, Romae: Jus Pontificium, 1927.

Turner, Sidney Joseph, *The Vow of Poverty,* The Catholic University of America, Canon Law Studies, No. 54, Washington, D. C.: The Catholic University of America, 1929.

Van Espen, Bernardus, *Ius Ecclesiasticum Universum,* 4 vols., Lovanii, 1753.

Vermeersch, Arthurus, *De Religiosis Institutis et Personis,* 4. ed., 2 vols., Brugis, 1907-1909.

Vermeersch, A.-Creusen, J., *Epitome Iuris Canonici,* 3 vols., Vol. I, 6. ed., Mechliniae et Romae: Dessain, 1937.

Vromant, G., *De Bonis Ecclesiae Temporalibus ad Usum praesertim Missionariorum et Religiosorum,* Louvain: Desbarax, 1927.

Wernz, Franciscus Xav.-Vidal, Petrus, *Ius Canonicum ad Codicis Normam Exactum,* 7 tomes in 9 vols., Tom. III *(De Religiosis),* Romae: Universitas Gregoriana, 1933.

Woywod, Stanislaus, *A Practical Commentary on the Code of Canon Law,* 3. ed., 2 vols., New York: Wagner, 1929.

Zallinger, J., *Institutiones Juris Ecclesiastici Maxime Privati, Ordine Decretalium,* Romae, 1823.

Periodicals

Apollinaris, Romae, 1928—

Analecta Juris Pontificii, Rome, 1852-1868; Paris, 1869-1890.

Archiv für katholisches Kirchenrecht, Innsbruck, 1857-1861; Mainz, 1862—

Commentarium pro Religiosis et Missionariis, Romae, 1920—

Jus Pontificium, Romae, 1921—

Periodica de Re Canonica et Morali utili Praesertim Religiosis et Missionariis, Bruges, 1905—

Revue des Communautés Religieuses, Louvain, 1925—

Theologie und Glaube, Paderborn, 1909—

Theologisch-praktische Quartalschrift, Linz, 1832—

Articles

Boudinhon, Augustus, "Dower," *Catholic Encyclopedia,* V, 146.

Creusen, J., "Restitution d'une dot,"—*Revue des Communautés Religieuses,* I (1925), 151-152.

———, "Placement des dots,"—*Revue des Communautés Religieuses,* II (1926), 185-186.

———, "Dispense de la dot,"—*Revue des Communautés Religieuses,* III (1927), 133.

————, "Administration d'une dot,"—*Revue des Communautés Religieuses,* VI (1930), 74-76.

D'Ambrosio, Franciscus Xav., "De Radicali Dominio Dotis Religiosarum in Institutis Iuris Pontificii,"—*Apollinaris,* I (1928), 173-176.

————, "De Dote Monialis ante Codicis Promulgationem Solemniter Professae et ad aliud Monasterium post Codicem Transeuntis,"— *Apollinaris,* I (1928), 297-300.

Eichmann, Eduard, "Die Dos der Klosterfrau,"—*Theologie und Glaube,* XXVI (1934), 161-176.

Fuchs, Vinzenz, "Rückgabe der Mitgift an die Ausscheidende Klosterfrau," —*ThPrQs,* LXXXVIII (1935), 359-368.

Goyeneche, S., "De Transitu ad aliam Religionem,"—*CpRM,* II (1921), 116-124.

————, "Consultationes,"—*CpRM,* V (1924), 161-163, and 390-393.

————, "Consultationes,"—*CpRM,* XI (1930), 36-38.

————, "Consultationes,"—*CpRM,* XIX (1938), 327-328.

————, "De Bonis Monialis ad aliud Monasterium Transeuntis,"—*CpRM,* XXI (1940), 38-40.

————, "Restitutio Dotis Religiosac Discedenti,"—*CpRM,* XX (1940), 36-38.

Jombart, E., "Une dot qui consisterait en une maison,"—*Revue des Communautés Religieuses,* I (1925), 157-159.

————, "Les dots,"—*Revue des Communautés Religieuses,* III (1927), 55-58.

Jone, Heribert, "Herausgabe der Mitgift Einer Ordensschwester,"—*ThPrQs,* LXXXII (1929), 133-136.

Larraona, Arcadius, "De Dote Religiosarum in Codice Juris Canonici,"— *CpRM,* XIX (1938), 19-30, and 93-99.

————, "Commentarium Codicis,"—*CpRM,* XX (1939), 8-17; 72-83; 146-155; 302-307; XXI (1940), 26-35; 79-83; 145-152; XIV (1933), 345-350.

Leinz, "Die Supernumerarier in den Klöstern,"—*AKKR.,* LXXIX (1899), 55-67.

Maroto, Philippus, "Annotationes,"—*CpRM,* V (1924), 321-323.

Steiger, A. P., "De Propagatione et Diffusione Vitae Religiosae,"— *Periodica,* XIII (1924), (29)-(52), and (73)-(100).

Vermeersch, A., "De Conscribendis Constitutionibus Congregationis Votorum Simplicium vel de iisdem ad Codicem Aptandis," II, 3, *De Dote,-* *Periodica,* XVI (1927), 156*.

[Vermeersch, A.?], "Facultatum quae, post Codicem, Legatis Apostolicis Concedi Consueverunt breve Commentarium," c. V, De Facultatibus circa Religiosos, n. 47—*Periodica,* XII (1923), (143)-(144).

————, "Varia Quaesita de Religiosis," c. III, De Dotis Quantitate Definienda,—*Periodica,* XII (1923), (162); c. V, De Attributione Bonorum Religiosi Transeuntis ad aliud Institutum—*Periodica,* XIV (1925), (49)-(51).

————, "De la dot des religieuses,"—*AJP,* IV (1860), 1525-1558.

AAS—Acta Apostolicae Sedis.
AJP—Analecta Juris Pontificii.
AKKR—Archiv für katholisches Kirchenrecht.
CpRM—Commentarium pro Religiosis et Missionariis.
Fontes—Codicis Iuris Canonici Fontes cura . . . Gasparri editi.
MPG—Migne, Patrologia, Series Graeca.
MPL—Migne, Patrologia, Series Latina.
Periodica—Periodica de Re Canonica et Morali utili Praesertim Religiosis et Missionariis.
S. C. C.—Sacra Congregatio Concilii.
S. C. de Rel.—Sacra Congregatio de Religiosis.
S. C. Ep. et Reg.—Sacra Congregatio Episcoporum et Regularium.
ThPrQs—Theologisch-praktische Quartalschrift.

BIOGRAPHICAL NOTE

THOMAS M. KEALY was born in Prosser, Nebraska, December 24, 1905. After completing his elementary school training in St. Cecilia's parochial school, Hastings, Nebraska, and his high school work in Hastings High School, he entered Hastings College, from which institution he received the degree of Bachelor of Arts in 1927. Entering St. Benedict's College, Atchison, Kansas, he began his philosophical course in the fall of 1928, continuing the following year at Kenrick Seminary, St. Louis, Mo., where he also completed his theological course. He was ordained to the priesthood March 31, 1934. Along with parochial assignments he served for four years as associate editor of the Lincoln diocesan newspaper, the *Southern Nebraska Register*. At the request of his Most Reverend Bishop he entered the Graduate School of Canon Law at the Catholic University in the fall of 1938. He received the degree of Bachelor of Canon Law in June 1939, and the degree of Licentiate of Canon Law in June 1940.

ALPHABETICAL INDEX

CANON LAW STUDIES

1. Freriks, Rev. Celestine A., C.PP.S., J.C.D., Religious Congregations in Their External Relations, 121 pp., 1916.
2. Galliher, Rev. Daniel M., O.P., J.C.D., Canonical Elections, 117 pp., 1917.
3. Borkowski, Rev. Aurelius L., O.F.M., J.C.D., De Confraternitatibus Ecclesiasticis, 136 pp., 1918.
4. Castillo, Rev. Cayo, J.C.D., Disertacion Historico-Canonica sobre la Potestad del Cabildo en Sede Vacante o Impedida del Vicario Capitular, 99 pp., 1919 (1918).
5. Kubelbeck, Rev. William J., S.T.B., J.C.D., The Sacred Pentitentiaria and Its Relations to Faculties of Ordinaries and Priests, 129 pp., 1918.
6. Petrovits, Rev. Joseph J. C., S.T.D., J.C.D., The New Church Law on Matrimony, X-461 pp., 1919.
7. Hickey, Rev. John J., S.T.B., J.C.D., Irregularities and Simple Impediments in the New Code of Canon Law, 100 pp., 1920.
8. Klekotka, Rev. Peter J., S.T.B., J.C.D., Diocesan Consultors, 179 pp., 1920.
9. Wanenmacher, Rev. Francis, J.C.D., The Evidence in Ecclesiastical Procedure Affecting the Marriage Bond, 1920 (Printed 1935).
10. Golden, Rev. Henry Francis, J.C.D., Parochial Benefices in the New Code, IV-119 pp., 1921 (Printed 1925).
11. Koudelka, Rev. Charles J., J.C.D., Pastors, Their Rights and Duties According to the New Code of Canon Law, 211 pp., 1921.
12. Melo, Rev. Antonius, O.F.M., J.C.D., De Exemptione Regularium, X-188 pp., 1921.
13. Schaaf, Rev. Valentine Theodore, O.F.M., S.T.B., J.C.D., The Cloister, X-180 pp., 1921.
14. Burke, Rev. Thomas Joseph, S.T.D., J.C.D., Competence in Ecclesiastical Tribunals, IV-117 pp., 1922.
15. Leech, Rev. George Leo, J.C.D., A Comparative Study of the Constitution, "Apostolicae Sedis" and the "Codex Juris Canonici," 179 pp., 1922.
16. Motry, Rev. Hubert Louis, S.T.D., J.C.D., Diocesan Faculties According to the Code of Canon Law, II-167 pp., 1922.
17. Murphy, Rev. George Lawrence, J.C.D., Delinquencies and Penalties in the Administration and Reception of the Sacraments, IV-121 pp., 1923.
18. O'Reilly, Rev. John Anthony, S.T.B., J.C.D., Ecclesiastical Sepulture in the New Code of Canon Law, II-129 pp., 1923.

19. Michalicka, Rev. Wenceslas Cyrill, O.S.B., J.C.D., Judicial Procedure in Dismissal of Clerical Exempt Religious, 107 pp., 1923.

20. Dargin, Rev. Edward Vincent, S.T.B., J.C.D., Reserved Cases According to the Code of Canon Law, IV-103 pp., 1924.

21. Godfrey, Rev. John A., S.T.B., J.C.D., The Right of Patronage According to the Code of Canon Law, 153 pp., 1924.

22. Hagedorn, Rev. Francis Edward, J.C.D., General Legislation on Indulgences, II-154 pp., 1924.

23. King, Rev. James Ignatius, J.C.D., The Administration of the Sacraments to Dying Non-Catholics, V-141 pp., 1924.

24. Winslow, Rev. Francis Joseph, A.F.M., J.C.D., Vicars and Prefects Apostolic, IV-149 pp., 1924.

25. Correa, Rev. Jose Servelion, S.T.L., J.C.D., La Potestad Legislativa de la Iglesia Catolica, IV-127 pp., 1925.

26. Dugan, Rev. Henry Francis, A.M., J.C.D., The Judiciary Department of the Diocesan Curia, 87 pp., 1925.

27. Keller, Rev. Charles Frederick, S.T.B., J.C.D., Mass Stipends, 167 pp., 1925.

28. Paschang, Rev. John Linus, J.C.D., The Sacramentals According to the Code of Canon Law, 129 pp., 1925.

29. Piontek, Rev. Cyrillus, O.F.M., S.T.B., J.C.D., De Indulto Exclaustrationis necnon Saecularizationis, XIII-289 pp., 1925.

30. Kearney, Rev. Richard Joseph, S.T.B., J.C.D., Sponsors at Baptism According to the Code of Canon Law, IV-127 pp., 1925.

31. Bartlett, Rev. Chester Joseph, A.M., LL.B., J.C.D., The Tenure of Parochial Property in the United States of America, V-108 pp., 1926.

32. Kilker, Rev. Adrian Jerome, J.C.D., Extreme Unction, V-425 pp., 1926.

33. McCormick, Rev. Robert Emmett, J.C.D., Confessors of Religious, VIII-266 pp., 1926.

34. Miller, Rev. Newton Thomas, J.C.D., Founded Masses According to the Code of Canon Law, VII-93 pp., 1926.

35. Roelker, Rev. Edward G., S.T.D., J.C.D., Principles of Privilege According to the Code of Canon Law, XI-166 pp., 1926.

36. Bakalarczyk, Rev. Richardus, M.I.C., J.U.D., De Novitiatu, VIII-208 pp., 1927.

37. Pizzuti, Rev. Lawrence, O.F.M., J.U.L., De Parochis Religiosis, 1927. (Not printed.)

38. Bliley, Rev. Nicholas Martin, O.S.B., J.C.D., Altars According to the Code of Canon Law, XIX-132 pp., 1927.

39. Brown, Mr. Brendan Francis, A.B., LL.M., J.U.D., The Canonical Juristic Personality with Special Reference to Its Status in the United States of America, V-212 pp., 1927.

40. Cavanaugh, Rev. William Thomas, C.P., J.U.D., The Reservation of the Blessed Sacrament, VIII-101 pp., 1927.

41. Doheny, Rev. William J., C.S.C., A.B., J.U.D., Church Property: Modes of Acquisition, X-118 pp., 1927.
42. Feldhaus, Rev. Aloysius H., C.PP.S., J.C.D., Oratories, IX-141 pp., 1927.
43. Kelly, Rev. James Patrick, A.B., J.C.D., The Jurisdiction of the Simple Confessor, X-208 pp., 1927.
44. Neuberger, Rev. Nicholas J., J.C.D., Canon 6 or the Relation of the Codex Juris Canonici to the Preceding Legislation, V-95 pp., 1927.
45. O'Keefe, Rev. Gerald Michael, J.C.D., Matrimonial Dispensations, Powers of Bishops, Priests and Confessors, VIII-232 pp., 1927.
46. Quigley, Rev. Joseph A. M., A.B., J.C.B., Condemned Societies, 139 pp., 1927.
47. Zaplotnik, Rev. Johannes Leo, J.C.D., De Vicariis Foraneis, X-142 pp., 1927.
48. Duskie, Rev. John Aloysius, A.B., J.C.D., The Canonical Status of the Orientals in the United States, VIII-196 pp., 1928.
49. Hyland, Rev. Francis Edward, J.C.D., Excommunication, Its Nature, Historical Development and Effects, VIII-181 pp., 1928.
50. Reinmann, Rev. Gerald Joseph, O.M.C., J.C.D., The Third Order Secular of Saint Francis, 201 pp., 1928.
51. Schenk, Rev. Francis J., J.C.D., The Matrimonial Impediments of Mixed Religion and Disparity of Cult, XVI-318 pp., 1929.
52. Coady, Rev. John Joseph, S.T.D., J.U.D., A.M., The Appointment of Pastors, VIII-150 pp., 1929.
53. Kay, Rev. Thomas Henry, J.C.D., Competence in Matrimonial Procedure, VIII-164 pp., 1929.
54. Turner, Rev. Sidney Joseph, C.P., J.U.D., The Vow of Poverty, XLIX-217 pp., 1929.
55. Kearney, Rev. Raymond A., A.B., S.T.D., J.C.D., The Principles of Delegation, VII-149 pp., 1929.
56. Conran, Rev. Edward James, A.B., J.C.D., The Interdict, V-163 pp., 1930.
57. O'Neil, Rev. William H., J.C.D., Papal Rescripts of Favor, VII-218 pp., 1930.
58. Bastnagel, Rev. Clement Vincent, J.U.D., The Appointment of Parochial Adjutants and Assistants, XV-257 pp., 1930.
59. Ferry, Rev. William A., A.B., J.C.D., Stole Fees, V-135 pp., 1930.
60. Costello, Rev. John Michael, A.B., J.C.D., Domicile and Quasi-domicile, VII-201 pp., 1930.
61. Kremer, Rev. Michael Nicholas, A.B., S.T.B., J.C.D., Church Support in the United States, VI-1930.
62. Angulo, Rev. Luis, C.M., J.C.D., Legislation de la Iglesia sobre la intencion en la application de la Santa Misa, VII-104 pp., 1931.
63. Frey, Rev. Wolfgang Norbert, O.S.B., A.B., J.C.D., The Act of Religious Profession, VIII-174 pp., 1931.

64. Roberts, Rev. James Brendan, A.B., J.C.D., The Banns of Marriage, XIV-140 pp., 1931.

65. Ryder, Rev. Raymond Aloysius, A.B., J.C.D., Simony, IX-151 pp., 1931.

66. Campagna, Rev. Angelo, Ph.D., J.U.D., Il Vicario Generale del Vescovo, VII-205 pp., 1931.

67. Cox, Rev. Joseph Godfrey, A.B., J.C.D., The Administration of Seminaries, VI-124 pp., 1931.

68. Gregory, Rev. Donald J., J.U.D., The Pauline Privilege, XV-165 pp., 1931.

69. Donohue, Rev. John F., J.C.D., The Impediment of Crime, VII-110 pp., 1931.

70. Dooley, Rev. Eugene A., O.M.I., J.C.D., Church Law on Sacred Relics, IX-143 pp., 1931.

71. Orth, Rev. Raymond Clement, O.M.C., J.C.D., The Approbation of Religious Institutes, 171 pp., 1931.

72. Pernicone, Rev. Joseph M., A.B., J.C.D., The Ecclesiastical Prohibition of Books, XII-267 pp., 1932.

73. Clinton, Rev. Connell, A.B., J.C.D., The Paschal Precept, IX-108 pp., 1932.

74. Donnelly, Rev. Francis B., A.M., S.T.L., J.C.D., The Diocesan Synod, VIII-125 pp., 1932.

75. Torrente, Rev. Camilo, C.M.F., J.C.D., Las Processiones Sagradas, V-145 pp., 1932.

76. Murphy, Rev. Edwin J., C.PP.S., J.C.D., Suspension Ex Informata Conscientia, XI-122 pp., 1932.

77. Mackenzie, Rev. Eric F., A.M., S.T.L., J.C.D., The Delict of Heresy in Its Commission, Penalization, Absolution, VII-124 pp., 1932.

78. Lyons, Rev. Avitus E., S.T.B., J.C.D., The Collegiate Tribunal of First Instance, XI-147 pp., 1932.

79. Connolly, Rev. Thomas A., J.C.D., Appeals, XI-195 pp., 1932.

80. Sangmeister, Rev. Joseph V., A.B., J.C.D., Force and Fear as Precluding Martimonial Consent, V-211 pp., 1932.

81. Jaeger, Rev. Leo A., A.B., J.C.D., The Administration of Vacant and Quasi-vacant Episcopal Sees in the United States, IX-229 pp., 1932.

82. Rimlinger, Rev. Herbert T., J.C.D., Error Invalidating Matrimonial Consent, VII-79 pp., 1932.

83. Barrett, Rev. John D. M., S.S., J.C.D., A Comparative Study of the Third Plenary Council of Baltimore and the Code, IX-221 pp., 1932.

84. Carberry, Rev. John J., Ph.D., S.T.D., J.C.D., The Juridical Form of Marriage, X-177 pp., 1934.

85. Dolan, Rev. John L., A.B., J.C.D., The Defensor Vinculi, XII-157 pp., 1934.

86. Hannan, Rev. Jerome D., A.M., S.T.D., LL.B., J.C.D., The Canon Law of Wills, IX-517 pp., 1934.

87. Lemieux, Rev. Delisle A., A.M., J.C.D., The Sentence in Ecclesiastical Procedure, IX-131 pp., 1934.

88. O'Rourke, Rev. James J., A.B., J.C.D., Parish Registers, VII-109 pp., 1934.

89. Timlin, Rev. Bartholomew, O.F.M., A.M., J.C.D., Conditional Matrimonial Consent, X-381 pp., 1934.

90. Wahl, Rev. Francis X., A.B., J.C.D., The Matrimonial Impediments of Consanguinity and Affinity, VI-125 pp., 1934.

91. White, Rev. Robert J., A.B., LL.B., S.T.B., J.C.D., Canonical Ante-Nuptial Promises and the Civil Law, VI-152 pp., 1934.

92. Herrera, Rev. Antonio Parra, O.C.D., J.C.D., Legislation Ecclesiastica sobra el Ayuno y la Abstinencia, XI-191 pp., 1935.

93. Kennedy, Rev. Edwin J., J.C.D., The Special Matrimonial Process in Cases of Evident Nullity, X-165 pp., 1935.

94. Manning, Rev. John J., A.B., J.C.D., Presumption of Law in Matrimonial Procedure, XI-111 pp., 1935.

95. Moeder, Rev. John M., J.C.D., The Proper Bishop for Ordination and Dismissorial Letters, VII-135 pp., 1935.

96. O'Mara, Rev. William A., A.B., J.C.D., Canonical Causes for Matrimonial Dispensations, IX-155 pp., 1935.

97. Reilly, Rev. Peter, J.C.D., Residence of Pastors, IX-81 pp., 1935.

98. Smith, Rev. Mariner T., O.P., S.T.L., J.C.D., The Penal Law for Religious, VII-169 pp., 1935.

99. Whalen, Rev. Donald W., A.M., J.C.D., The Value of Testimonial Evidence in Matrimonial Procedure, XIII-297 pp., 1935.

100. Cleary, Rev. Joseph F., J.C.D., Canonical Limitations on the Alienation of Church Property, VIII-141 pp., 1936.

101. Glynn, Rev. John C., J.C.D., The Promoter of Justice, XX-337 pp., 1936.

102. Brennan, Rev. James H., S.S., A.M., S.T.B., J.C.D., The Simple Convalidation of Marriage, VI-135 pp., 1937.

103. Brunini, Rev. Joseph Bernard, J.C.D., The Clerical Obligations of Canons 139 and 142, X-121 pp., 1937.

104. Connor, Rev. Maurice, A.B., J.C.D., The Administrative Removal of Pastors, VIII-159 pp., 1937.

105. Guilfoyle, Rev. Merlin Joseph, J.C.D., Custom, XI-144 pp., 1937.

106. Hughes, Rev. James Austin, A.B., A.M., J.C.D., Witnesses in Criminal Trials of Clerics, IX-140 pp., 1937.

107. Jansen, Rev. Raymond J., A.B., S.T.L., J.C.D., Canonical Provisions for Catechetical Instruction, VII-153 pp., 1937.

108. Kealy, Rev. John James, A.B., J.C.D., The Introductory Libellus in Church Court Procedure, XI-121 pp., 1937.

109. McManus, Rev. James Edward, C.SS.R., J.C.D., The Administration of Temporal Goods in Religious Institutes, XVI-196 pp., 1937.

110. Moriarity, Rev. Eugene James, J.C.D., Oaths in Ecclesiastical Courts, X-115 pp., 1937.
111. Rainer, Rev. Eligius George, C.SS.R., J.C.D., Suspension of Clerics, XVII-249 pp., 1937.
112. Reilly, Rev. Thomas F., C.SS.R., J.C.D., Visitation of Religious, VI-195 pp., 1938.
113. Moriarty, Rev. Francis E., C.SS.R., J.C.D., The Extraordinary Absolution from Censures, XV-334 pp., 1938.
114. Connolly, Rev. Nicholas P., J.C.D., The Canonical Erection of Parishes, X-132 pp., 1938.
115. Donovan, Rev. James Joseph, J.C.D., The Pastor's Obligation in Prenuptial Investigation, XII-322 pp., 1938.
116. Harrigan, Rev. Robert J., M.A., S.T.B., J.C.D., The Radical Sanation of Invalid Marriages, VIII-208 pp., 1938.
117. Boffa, Rev. Conrad Humbert, J.C.D., Canonical Provisions for Catholic Schools, X-211 pp., 1939.
118. Parsons, Rev. Anscar John, O.F.M. Cap., J.C.D., Canonical Elections, XII-236 pp., 1939.
119. Reilly, Rev. Edward Michael, A.B., J.C.D., The General Norms of Dispensation, X-156 pp., 1939.
120. Ryan, Rev. Gerald Aloysius, A.B., J.C.D., Principles of Episcopal Jurisdiction, XII-172 pp., 1939.
121. Burton, Rev. Francis James, C.S.C., A.B., J.C.D., A Commentary on Canon 1125, X-212 pp., 1940.
122. Miaskiewicz, Rev. Francis Sigismund, J.C.D., Supplied Jurisdiction According to Canon 209, XII-340 pp., 1940.
123. Rice, Rev. Patrick William, A.B., J.C.D., Proof of Death in Prenuptial Investigation, VII-156 pp., 1940.
124. Anglin, Rev. Thomas Francis, M.S., J.C.L., The Eucharistic Fast.
125. Coleman, Rev. John Jerome, J.C.L., The Minister of Confirmation.
126. Downs, Rev. John Emmanuel, A.B., J.C.L., The Concept of Clerical Immunity.
127. Esswein, Rev. Anthony Albert, J.C.L., Extrajudicial Penal Powers of Ecclesiastical Superiors.
128. Farrell, Rev. Benjamin Francis, M.A., S.T.L., J.C.L., The Rights and Duties of the Local Ordinary Regarding Congregations of Women Religious of Pontifical Approval.
129. Feeney, Rev. Thomas John, A.B., S.T.L., J.C.L., Restitutio in Integrum.
130. Findlay, Rev. Stephen William, O.S.B., A.B., J.C.L., Canonical Norms Governing the Deposition and Degradation of Clerics.
131. Goodwine, Rev. John, A.B., S.T.L., J.C.L., The Right of the Church to Acquire Property.
132. Heston, Rev. Edward Louis, C.S.C., Ph.D., S.T.D., J.C.L., The Alienation of Church Property in the United States.

133. Hogan, Rev. James John, S.T.L., J.C.L., Judicial Advocates and Procurators.
134. Kealy, Rev. Thomas M., A.B., Litt.B., J.C.L., Dowry of Women Religious.
135. Keene, Rev. Michael James, O.S.B., J.C.L., Religious Ordinaries and Canon 198.
136. Kerin, Rev. Charles A., S.S., M.A., S.T.B., J.C.L., The Privation of Christian Burial.
137. Louis, Rev. William Francis, M.A., J.C.L., Diocesan Archives.
138. McDevitt, Rev. Gilbert Joseph, A.B., J.C.L., Legitimacy and Legitimation.
139. McDonough, Rev. Thomas Joseph, A.B., J.C.L., Apostolic Administrators.
140. Meier, Rev. Carl Anthony, A.B., J.C.L., Penal Administrative Procedure Against Negligent Pastors.
141. Schmidt, Rev. John Rogg, A.B., J.C.L., The Principles of Authentic Interpretation in Canon 17 of the Code of Canon Law.
142. Slafkosky, Rev. Andrew Leonard, A.B., J.C.L., The Canonical Episcopal Visitation of the Diocese.
143. Swoboda, Rev. Innocent Robert, O.F.M., J.C.L., Ignorance in Relation to the Imputability of Delicts.
144. Dube, Rev. Arthur Joseph, A.B., J.C.L., The General Principles for the Reckoning of Time in Canon Law.
145. McBride, Rev. James T., A.B., J.C.L., Incardination and Excardination of Seculars.